Contents

I0015105

~ Welcome & What You'll Learn

Section 5: Hands-On Project - Rusty ToDo List (A simple command-line ToDo list application)

~ Conclusion

Welcome & What You'll Learn

Welcome to the exciting world of Rust programming! If you're searching for a language that prioritizes speed, reliability, and safety without sacrificing power and expressiveness, you've at the perfect place. Rust has established a firm foothold in the hearts of developers and companies alike, thanks to its unique approach to memory management and its unwavering focus on preventing errors before your code even runs.

Why You Should Dive into Rust

Let's explore some of the compelling reasons why Rust should be on your radar:

- **Performance:** Rust code effortlessly rivals the speed of languages like C and C++, making it an outstanding choice for projects demanding lightning-fast execution.
- **Memory Safety:** Rust's core strength lies in its compiler-enforced memory safety. Say goodbye to frustrating memory-related errors such as buffer overflows, dangling pointers, and data races that plague traditional languages.
- **Concurrency Confidence:** Rust arms you with powerful tools to write concurrent code fearlessly, ensuring multi-threaded programs behave exactly as you intend them to.
- **Developer Delight:** Rust enjoys an enthusiastic and supportive community, along with exceptional tooling and clear, concise documentation. The language is designed to empower you, not hinder you.
- **Versatility:** Rust excels in a wide array of domains, from systems programming, web development, and game development to embedded systems, network programming, and more.

The "Fast-Track" Promise

"Rust Programming: A Fast-Track Guide" is your tailored expedition into this compelling programming language. We recognize your time is precious, which is why this book is built from the ground up to help you master the fundamentals of Rust and start building meaningful projects with confidence in record time.

What This Book Offers

Here's a glimpse into the carefully crafted journey that awaits you:

- **Step-by-Step Foundation:** We begin by introducing core concepts and the principles governing the Rust ecosystem. You'll get a firm grasp of Rust's syntax, building blocks, and the essential tools used by Rust developers.
- **Memory Mastery:** We'll unravel Rust's innovative ownership and borrowing models. These form the backbone of its safety guarantees and will empower you to manage memory with unprecedented precision.
- **Type Triumphs:** Discover the intricacies of Rust's type system and how to work effectively with its various data structures to represent and manipulate your program's data.
- **Practical Projects:** The knowledge you acquire will be cemented through hands-on projects. Our 'Rusty ToDo' List project will guide you from its foundations to a fully functional command-line application.
- **Best Practices:** Throughout the book, we'll emphasize proven design patterns and idiomatic Rust code to help you write not only functional programs but beautifully structured and maintainable ones.

Ready to Begin?

If you're ready to embark on a journey that blends speed, safety, and elegant design, this book is for you. Whether you're an experienced programmer looking to broaden your skills or a newcomer to the programming landscape, Rust has something remarkable to offer everyone.

Let's turn the page and start our Rust adventure!

Additional Resources

- **The Rust Programming Language (The Rust Book):**
  https://doc.rust-lang.org/book/
- **Rust By Example:** https://doc.rust-lang.org/rust-by-example/
- **Rust Playground:** https://play.rust-lang.org/

Section 1:
Mastering Fundamentals

Navigating Cargo: Setting Sail into Rust

Welcome aboard! In this chapter, we'll embark on a journey with Rust's essential companion, Cargo. It's more than just a package manager; Cargo is your ship's navigator, construction foreman, and automation expert all rolled into one. Let's chart a course to understand its role and how to skillfully maneuver within the Rust development ecosystem.

What is Cargo?

At its core, Cargo performs three primary functions:

1. **Dependency Management:** Cargo streamlines finding, downloading, and compiling the libraries (known as 'crates' in the Rust world) upon which your project depends.
2. **Build System:** With simple commands, Cargo orchestrates the compilation of your Rust code, ensuring everything is assembled correctly.
3. **Project Scaffolding:** Cargo jumpstarts your projects by generating a standard Rust project structure, saving you valuable setup time.

The Heart of a Rust Project: Cargo.toml

Each Rust project contains a `Cargo.toml` file. Think of it as your ship's manifest - it outlines your project's details and instructions for Cargo. Here's a breakdown of its key sections:

- **[package]** Metadata about your project: name, version, authors, and more.
- **[dependencies]** A list of external crates your project relies upon, along with their version requirements.

Everyday Cargo Commands

Let's familiarize ourselves with essential Cargo commands that you'll use time and again:

- `cargo new project_name`: Creates a new Rust project with a basic directory structure and `Cargo.toml`.
- `cargo build`: Compiles your project.
- `cargo run`: Compiles your project (if necessary) and then executes the resulting program.
- `cargo check`: Performs a quick compilation without producing an executable, ideal for catching errors rapidly during development.
- `cargo test` Runs your project's test suite.
- `cargo doc` Generates comprehensive documentation for your project's code.

Adding Dependencies

Let's say you want to incorporate a crate like 'rand' (for random number generation) into your project. Here's how:

1. **Edit `Cargo.toml`:** Under the `[dependencies]` section, add a line like:

```
rand = "0.8.5"
```

2. **Build Your Project:** Run `cargo build`. Cargo will automatically fetch the 'rand' crate and its dependencies, compiling them alongside your code.

The Power of crates.io

Crates.io (https://crates.io/) is Rust's official package registry, a treasure trove of open-source libraries ready to empower your projects. Explore, search, and discover crates to add fantastic functionality to your Rust adventures.

Setting Sail with Confidence

Cargo is an indispensable tool in your Rust development journey. By mastering its basic commands, managing dependencies, and understanding the structure of `Cargo.toml`, you establish a strong foundation for navigating the exciting waters of Rust programming.

Additional Resources

- **The Cargo Book:** https://doc.rust-lang.org/cargo/
- **Crates.io:** https://crates.io/

Onwards!

With Cargo as your guide, you're well-equipped to streamline project setup, harness the power of external libraries, and build your Rust projects with ease. Let's continue the journey and explore more of Rust's fundamental building blocks.

Harnessing Cargo's Power: Advanced Project Management

In the previous chapter, we set sail with Cargo, learning about its fundamental roles. Now, let's navigate deeper and discover advanced techniques to manage our Rust projects with precision and efficiency.

Workspaces: Managing Multi-Crate Projects

Rust workspaces offer an elegant solution when your project encompasses multiple interconnected crates. Here's how you would structure a workspace:

```
[workspace]
members = [
    "project_a",
    "project_b",
]
```

- **Benefits:**
    - Unified dependency management: Updates across crates are streamlined.
    - Consolidated builds: Compile all your workspace crates with a single `cargo build` command.
    - Shared testing: Write tests spanning multiple crates within the workspace.

Features: Conditional Compilation

Rust's 'features' mechanism is analogous to optional spices you add to a dish – they enable you to tailor your project's build based on specific conditions. Consider this `Cargo.toml` snippet:

```
[dependencies]
super_database = { version = "1.0", optional = true
}
crypto_utils = { version = "0.5", optional = true }

[features]
database = ["super_database"]
encryption = ["crypto_utils"]
```

- **Using features:**

- ○ At build time: `cargo build --features "database encryption"`
- ○ In your code:

```
#[cfg(feature = "database")]
 pub fn connect_to_database() { … }
```

Custom Build Scripts (`build.rs`)

For fine-grained control over your build process, create a `build.rs` file at the root of your project. This Rust file is executed by Cargo before compilation. Use cases include:

- Code generation
- Compiling non-Rust code (like C libraries)
- Special file handling or setup tasks

Example `build.rs`:

```
fn main() {
    println!("cargo:rerun-if-changed=resources/");
}
```

This simple script signals Cargo to rebuild if anything changes in the 'resources' directory.

Profiles: Optimize for Purpose

Cargo profiles empower you to customize build configurations for different scenarios (e.g., development vs. release). Modify your `Cargo.toml`:

```
[profile.dev]
opt-level = 0 # Prioritize debugging ease

[profile.release]
opt-level = 3 # Aggressive performance optimization
```

- **Using profiles:** `cargo build --profile release`

Tips & Tricks

- **Overriding Dependencies:** Temporarily use a different version of a dependency for testing or a specific branch from a git repository.
- **Workspace-level Targets:** Define custom scripts or executables at the workspace level, shared across your crates.

The Power in Your Hands

By harnessing features, workspaces, build scripts, and profiles, you gain remarkable flexibility to manage the complexities of your Rust projects. These tools let you adapt your build processes, achieve conditional compilation, and optimize for various environments.

Additional Resources

- **Cargo Workspaces:**
  https://doc.rust-lang.org/cargo/reference/workspaces.html
- **Cargo Features:**
  https://doc.rust-lang.org/cargo/reference/features.html
- **Cargo Build Scripts:**
  https://doc.rust-lang.org/cargo/reference/build-scripts.html
- **Cargo Profiles:**
  https://doc.rust-lang.org/cargo/reference/profiles.html

Next Up: Unlocking Variables

Let's move forward and explore the intricacies of variables, the fundamental building blocks for storing and manipulating data in Rust.

Unraveling Variables: Foundations of Rust's Data Management

Variables are like labeled boxes in your computer's memory. They give names to values and allow us to store, modify, and reuse data throughout our Rust programs. Rust's approach to variables is entwined with its emphasis on safety and predictability.

Declaring Variables: The `let` Keyword

In Rust, we introduce variables using the `let` keyword:

```rust
let score = 100;
let is_active = true;
let player_name = "Alice";
```

- **Mutability:** By default, variables in Rust are immutable. This means, once a value is bound to a variable, it cannot be changed. We'll explore mutability in depth later.

Type Inference: Rust to the Rescue

Rust is usually smart enough to determine the data type of your variable based on its initial value. This is called type inference:

```rust
let level = 5;       // Rust infers 'level' is an integer
let progress = 0.75; // Rust infers 'progress' is a floating-point number
```

Explicit Type Annotations

There might be times you want to be more specific about a variable's type. Use a colon (`:`) after the variable name, followed by the type:

```rust
let character_code: u32 = 65; // 'u32' for 32-bit unsigned integer
let message: &str = "Hello!"; // '&str' for a string slice
```

Key Points: Variable Naming

- Names are case-sensitive (playerHealth is different from playerhealth)
- Convention is 'snake_case' (lowercase with underscores)
- Names should be descriptive

Shadowing: Reusing Variable Names

Rust allows a unique concept called 'shadowing'. You can redeclare a variable with the same name within a different scope:

```
let x = 10;

{
  let x = "Hello"; // Shadows outer 'x' - this 'x'
is a string
  println!("Inner x: {}", x);
}

println!("Outer x: {}", x); // Original 'x' (the
number) is back
```

Shadowing is often used to change a variable's type while maintaining clarity.

Constants: Values Set in Stone

For values that should never change throughout your program, use constants:

```
const MAX_SPEED: u16 = 255;
```

- Naming convention: all uppercase with underscores
- Must have an explicit type annotation
- Value must be known at compile time

Understanding Immutability

Rust's default immutability promotes predictability and helps prevent accidental data corruption. It might feel restrictive initially, but you'll soon appreciate the safety net it provides, and there are ways to achieve changes safely when needed.

Next Up: Deep-Diving into Variables

In our next chapter, we'll take a closer look at variable manipulation, exploring how to work with data effectively within the bounds of Rust's principles.

Additional Resources

- **Variables and Mutability:**
  https://doc.rust-lang.org/book/ch03-01-variables-and-mutability.html
- **Data Types:**
  https://doc.rust-lang.org/book/ch03-02-data-types.html
- **Constants:**
  https://doc.rust-lang.org/reference/items/constant-items.html

Delving Deeper into Variables: Advanced Techniques for Data Manipulation

In the previous chapter, we laid the foundation for understanding variables and their role in Rust. Now, let's unlock more nuanced techniques to manage and transform data effectively.

Mutability: When Change Is Necessary

Recall that by default, variables in Rust are immutable. To enable modification, we introduce the mut keyword during declaration:

```
let mut count = 0;
```

```
count += 1;   // Now we can modify the value of
'count'
```

Tips for Mutability

- Use it judiciously: Immutability is your ally for safer code; employ `mut` strategically only when truly needed.
- Limit scope: Minimize the sections of code where a variable is mutable to retain control.

Moving Values: Ownership in Action

Rust's ownership system can sometimes lead to unexpected behavior when dealing with variables of certain types:

```
let msg1 = String::from("Hello");
let msg2 = msg1; // msg1 is no longer valid!
```

Under the hood, a move has occurred, transferring ownership of the underlying string data from `msg1` to `msg2`. Trying to use `msg1` would now result in an error.

Copying vs. Moving

- **Scalar types** (integers, booleans, etc.): Generally copied by default, creating duplicate values.
- **Complex types** (like `String`): Moved by default to avoid potentially expensive memory operations.

Cloning: For Explicit Copies

If you need a true copy of a value, use the `.clone()` method:

```
let msg1 = String::from("Hello");
let msg2 = msg1.clone();   // Full copy, both msg1
and msg2 usable
```

Be aware that `clone()` can sometimes be a slower operation, especially with large data structures.

Stack vs. Heap: A Quick Detour

- **Stack:** Quick, fixed-size memory for scalar values.
- **Heap:** Slower, flexible memory for dynamic data (like the content of String). Moves generally involve simple stack updates, while copies might necessitate heap operations.

Destructuring: Extracting Values from Structures

Let's say you have a tuple:

```
let coordinates = (32.4, -105.7);
let x = coordinates.0;
let y = coordinates.1;
```

Destructuring offers a cleaner way to unpack values:

```
let (x, y) = coordinates;
```

Advanced Destructuring: You can destructure structs, enums, and even use patterns for complex data extraction. Explore this further!

The Freezing Effect: Immutability within Structures

Even if parts of a structure are mutable, the concept of immutability extends to how you interact with the structure if it's initially declared immutable.

```
struct Player {
    name: String,
    score: i32,
}

let player = Player { name: "Bob".to_string(),
score: 0 };
//player.name = "Alice".to_string(); // Error:
cannot modify part of an immutable struct
```

To change a field, you would need to either declare the entire structure as mutable or explore other techniques we'll cover in later chapters on structs.

Beyond the Basics

We've just scratched the surface of advanced variable manipulation in Rust. As you progress, you'll encounter even more powerful tools, including references and borrowing, which offer highly controlled ways to share data without full ownership transfers.

Additional Resources

- **Ownership:**
  https://doc.rust-lang.org/book/ch04-01-what-is-ownership.html
- **Structs:**
  https://doc.rust-lang.org/book/ch05-01-defining-structs.html
- **Destructuring:**
  https://doc.rust-lang.org/book/ch18-03-pattern-syntax.html#destructuring-to-break-apart-values

Exploring Scope: Mapping Your Rust Terrain

The Essence of Scope

Scope defines:

- **Accessibility:** Which parts of your code can use a particular variable or function.
- **Lifetime:** How long a variable remains valid before being automatically cleaned up.

Block Scope: The Building Blocks

In Rust, curly braces { } define a block scope. Variables declared within a block are only accessible inside that block and its nested sub-blocks.

```rust
fn main() {
    let outer_var = "Hello";

    {  // Start of a new block scope
        let inner_var = "World";
        println!("Inside block: {}, {}", outer_var,
inner_var);
    } // End of the block scope

    // println!("Outside block: {}", inner_var); //
Error! 'inner_var' not in scope
}
```

Scopes Within Functions

Functions create their own scopes. Variables declared within a function are confined to that function:

```rust
fn print_message() {
    let message = "Greetings!";
    println!("{}", message);
}

// message cannot be used outside the print_message
function
```

Shadowing Revisited

Recall that shadowing allows you to reuse a variable name within nested scopes. While the outer variable is temporarily hidden, its value remains unchanged:

```rust
let color = "blue";

{
```

```
    let color = "green"; // New 'color' variable for
inner block
    println!("Inner color: {}", color);
  }

println!("Outer color: {}", color);  // Original
'color' is restored
```

Scope, Ownership, and Lifetimes

Rust's ownership rules come into play with scope. When a variable goes out of scope, its value is dropped (cleaned from memory) if it owns that value. This is part of Rust's mechanism to prevent memory errors.

Tips & Tricks

- **Keep scopes small:** Smaller scopes improve code readability and limit the potential for naming conflicts.
- **Choose descriptive names:** Clear naming helps distinguish variables even when shadowing occurs.
- **Be mindful of variable lifetimes:** Design your code considering when Rust will automatically release resources.

Scope Within Control Flow

Variables declared within control flow structures (`if`, `for`, `while`) have scope limited to the branches of that structure. This can occasionally lead to desired behavior and sometimes, small surprises - it's something to keep in mind!

Moving Forward: Extending Scope

In our next chapter, we'll delve into situations where extending the lifetime of variables is necessary and explore some of the advanced techniques Rust offers to manage this in a controlled manner.

Additional Resources

- **A Gentle Introduction to Rust Scope:**
  https://doc.rust-lang.org/stable/rust-by-example/scope.html
- **Scope and Shadowing in Rust:**
  https://doc.rust-lang.org/book/ch03-01-variables-and-mutability.html#variable-scope

---

Extending Scope: Advanced Scenarios in Rust's Scope Management

Sometimes Rust's rules around variable lifetimes can feel a bit restrictive. There are instances where you legitimately need a value to persist beyond its typical block scope. Let's carefully examine the primary methods to achieve this, making sure we maintain the safety guarantees Rust is known for.

Scenario 1: Returning Values from Blocks

Consider the following function; it might not do exactly what you intended:

```
fn find_longer_string(str1: &str, str2: &str) ->
&str {
    if str1.len() > str2.len() {
        str1
    } else {
        str2
    }
}
```

The problem is that both `str1` and `str2` references will outlive the `find_longer_string` function scope. The returned reference would point to deallocated memory, a recipe for disaster! We need ways to manage this.

Techniques for Scope Extension

1. **Ownership Transfer:** When feasible, returning the value itself avoids lifetime issues, transferring ownership to the caller. If the caller no longer needs it, eventual cleanup is expected.
2. **Cloning:** If you need the original value within the function *and* want to return a copy, use `.clone()`. Remember, cloning may incur performance costs, especially for large data.
3. **References & Lifetimes:** Rust's borrowing system, which we'll delve into later, offers precise control. It allows you to create references with explicitly defined lifetimes preventing dangling references.

Scenario 2: Threading

When you spawn a new thread, its environment has its own scope. You can't directly pass variables by value to a thread as their original copies might expire before the thread uses them.

Solutions include:

- **move Closures:** Move ownership into a thread's closure for variables the thread needs exclusively.
- **Smart Pointers (Arc, Rc)** Designed for shared ownership scenarios among threads. (We'll discuss these later.)

Scenario 3: Closures

Closures can 'capture' variables from their enclosing scope. However, Rust's default behavior can be overly conservative. Careful use of move closures and considering reference types can help close the gap where needed.

Important Reminders

- **Rust prioritizes safety:** The compiler's strictness around scope is a protection mechanism, aiding you in writing more error-resistant code.
- **Choose wisely:** Scope extension techniques incur trade-offs, whether it's potential memory copying or the complexities of working with references.
- **The journey continues:** Upcoming chapters on references, borrowing, and smart pointers will arm you with even more robust tools for managing lifetimes and sharing data safely.

Additional Resources

- **Rust References and Lifetimes:**
  https://doc.rust-lang.org/book/ch10-03-lifetime-syntax.html
- **Smart Pointers in the Rust Book:**
  https://doc.rust-lang.org/book/ch15-00-smart-pointers.html

Let's continue!

Our next stop is a deep dive into the core pillar of Rust's safety – memory management. It will tie closely into these lifetime and scope concepts.

Safeguarding Memory: The Pillars of Rust's Safety Net

Traditional programming languages like C and C++ place substantial responsibility on you, the programmer, to meticulously manage memory allocation and deallocation. This complexity is a breeding ground for notorious bugs:

- **Memory leaks:** Forgetting to free memory leads to it being occupied but unused, potentially causing programs to exhaust resources and crash.
- **Dangling pointers:** References that point to deallocated memory, leading to unpredictable and catastrophic crashes when used.
- **Buffer overflows:** Writing data beyond allocated bounds, corrupting adjacent memory, and often exploited for security attacks.

Rust's Revolution: Safety Without Sacrifice

Rust's bold promise is eliminating entire *classes* of these common memory-related errors—all without resorting to a garbage collector (which adds its own performance implications). This is achieved through its core pillars:

1. Ownership

- Every value in Rust has a single owner.
- When the owner goes out of scope, the value is automatically dropped (cleaned up).
- No more double frees or dangling pointers!

Example:

```
fn main() {
    let my_string = String::from("hello"); //
my_string owns the data
    process_data(my_string);
    // my_string is no longer valid here (ownership
was moved to process_data)
}
```

2. Borrowing

- Rust allows you to temporarily 'borrow' values with references (&).
- The compiler enforces strict rules on references to prevent data races and invalidation:
  - You can have multiple read-only references (&) *or* a single mutable reference (&mut) at a given time.

Example:

```
fn print_length(text: &str) {
    println!("Length: {}", text.len());
}
```

3. Lifetimes

- An advanced system (which we'll explore further in a later chapter) allowing the compiler to track and validate reference validity, preventing the use of references that might outlive the data they point to.

The Rust Advantage

- **Error Prevention at Compile Time:** Rust's compiler is notoriously thorough. The ownership and borrowing rules are verified *before* your code runs, turning many potential runtime disasters into compile-time errors.
- **Freedom from Garbage Collection:** No unpredictable pauses in your application caused by a garbage collector kicking in.
- **Performance:** Rust's memory safety doesn't come at the cost of speed. It's on par with languages like C and C++.

Key Points

- **Initial Learning Curve:** Understanding ownership and borrowing takes some adjustment, especially if you come from traditional languages.
- **The Reward:** The initial investment pays off in more robust and predictable code, saving you debugging nightmares.

Next: Crafting Functions

With a solid grasp of memory management, let's explore how to build well-structured functions, the fundamental building blocks of modular Rust programs.

Additional Resources

- **Rust's Ownership Model:**
  https://doc.rust-lang.org/book/ch04-00-understanding-ownership.html
- **References and Borrowing:**
  https://doc.rust-lang.org/book/ch04-02-references-and-borrowing.html

---

Crafting Functions: Building Blocks of Rust's Logic

The humble function is a mighty tool. It allows you to encapsulate a specific task or computation, breaking your program into manageable and self-contained units.

Anatomy of a Rust Function

```
fn function_name(parameter1: type1, parameter2:
type2) -> return_type {
    // Function body: code to be executed
}
```

Let's break it down:

- **fn**: The keyword to declare a function.
- **function_name**: A descriptive name, typically using snake_case.
- **parameters**: Inputs to the function, separated by commas, with each parameter having a specified type.
- **-> return_type**: Specifies the type of value the function returns. If nothing is returned, this is omitted.
- **{ /* Function body */ }**: The code within the curly braces is executed when the function is called.

Example

```rust
fn calculate_area(length: i32, width: i32) -> i32 {
    length * width  // Implicitly returned
}
```

Calling Functions

To use a function, you call it by its name, providing arguments:

```rust
let area = calculate_area(5, 10);
 println!("The area is: {}", area);
```

Benefits of Functions

- **Code Reusability:** A well-defined function can be called from multiple places in your code, reducing redundancy.
- **Modularity:** Functions decompose your program into logical chunks, improving readability and organization.
- **Abstraction:** Functions hide implementation details, allowing you to modify their internals without breaking code that uses them.
- **Testing:** Smaller functions are much easier to test in isolation.

Function Parameters: Passing Information

Parameters act as placeholders for values passed into the function when it's called. In Rust, passing values generally involves either ownership transfer or borrowing (which we'll cover in later chapters in depth!)

Function Return Values: Sending Results Back

Functions can return a single value using the -> notation and the return keyword:

```rust
fn is_even(number: u32) -> bool {
    return number % 2 == 0;
}
```

Tips for Effective Functions

- **Keep them focused:** A function should ideally have a single, well-defined responsibility.
- **Choose descriptive names:** The name should clearly indicate what the function does.
- **Consider scope:** Carefully control the visibility of functions to enhance code organization.

Additional Resources

- **Functions in the Rust Book:** https://doc.rust-lang.org/book/ch03-03-how-functions-work.html

---

Fine-Tuning Functions: Advanced Strategies for Code Structure

In the previous chapter, we laid the groundwork for creating functions. Now, let's sharpen our skills and explore ways to enhance their design.

Default Parameters: Providing Flexibility

You can define default values for function parameters, making them optional:

```rust
fn greet(name: &str, greeting: &str = "Hello") {
    println!("{}, {}", greeting, name);
}


// Both of these calls are valid:
greet("Sarah", "Hi");              // Uses a custom
greeting
```

```
greet("Michael");                    // Uses the default
"Hello"
```

Optional Parameters with Option

Rust's Option type, which we'll cover in more detail later, is perfect for representing truly optional parameters:

```
fn calculate_area(length: i32, width: Option<i32>)
-> i32 {
    match width {
        Some(w) => length * w,
        None => length * length, // Assume a square
if width is not provided
    }
}
```

Variadic Functions: Handling Variable Arguments

(This is a slightly more advanced concept.) Special syntax lets you create functions accepting an arbitrary number of arguments:

```
fn sum(numbers: &[i32]) -> i32 {
    let mut total = 0;
    for num in numbers {
        total += num;
    }
    total
}
```

```
println!("Sum: {}", sum(&[10, 20, 35]));
```

Error Handling: Using the Result Type

Functions are prime candidates for signaling errors. The Result type lets you return either a successful value or an error:

```rust
use std::io::Error; // Import the I/O error type

fn read_data(filename: &str) -> Result<String,
Error> {
    // ... code to read data from a file
}
```

Function Pointers: Functions as Values

In Rust, functions are also first-class citizens. You can store them in variables and pass them to other functions (enabling concepts in functional programming):

```rust
fn do_twice(f: fn(i32) -> i32, arg: i32) -> i32 { //
f is a function pointer
    f(f(arg))
}

fn add_one(x: i32) -> i32 { x + 1 }

let result = do_twice(add_one, 5);
println!("Result: {}", result);
```

Beyond the Basics

Our exploration of function refinement continues. In upcoming chapters, we'll delve into:

- **Closures:** Mastering these powerful constructs for function-like behavior with captured environments.
- **Methods:** Learn how to associate functions with structs, creating object-oriented behaviors.

Additional Resources

- **Variadic Functions:**
  https://doc.rust-lang.org/stable/rust-by-example/fn/variadic.html

- **Function Pointers:**
  https://doc.rust-lang.org/stable/rust-by-example/fn.html
- **The Result Type:** https://doc.rust-lang.org/std/result/

Unveiling the Module System: Organising Your Rust World

As your Rust programs grow, it becomes essential to divide your code into logically cohesive units. Modules provide the perfect way to achieve this, promoting code reusability, maintainability, and clear separation of concerns.

What Is a Module?

A module is a collection of Rust code items: functions, structs, enums, constants, etc. Think of it as a self-contained package with its own namespace, controlling what is made visible outside the module.

Defining Modules

You can create modules directly within your Rust source files using the mod keyword:

```
mod my_math_module {
    pub fn add(a: i32, b: i32) -> i32 {
        a + b
    }

    fn subtract(a: i32, b: i32) -> i32 { // Private
function
        a - b
    }
```

```
    // ... more code ...
}

fn main() {
    let result = my_math_module::add(10, 5);
    println!("The sum is: {}", result);
}
```

Key Points

- **pub Keyword:** Items marked with pub are publicly accessible from outside the module. Items without pub remain private.
- **Module Tree:** Modules can be nested within other modules, forming a hierarchical structure.

Modules and Files

There are ways to organize modules across multiple files:

1. **Module in the Same File as main.rs:** Demonstrated in the previous example. Perfect for smaller modules.
2. **Dedicated File:** Create a separate file (my_math_module.rs) and declare the module within it.
3. **Directory as Module:** Create a directory (my_math_module) with a file named mod.rs inside. This mod.rs file contains the module content.

Bringing Modules into Scope: The use Keyword

To use items from a module, you bring them into scope with use:

```
use my_math_module::add; // Import the 'add'
function

fn main() {
    let result = add(20, 30);
    // ...
}
```

The Power of Namespacing

Modules prevent name collisions. You could have multiple add functions in different modules without conflict.

Benefits of Modules

- **Organization:** Break down complex projects into manageable chunks.
- **Encapsulation:** Hide implementation details, promoting a clear interface for module users.
- **Reusability:** Modules can be shared between projects.
- **Testing:** Isolates code for easier unit testing.

Crates and Modules

Recall that a Rust 'crate' is the fundamental compilation unit (a library or a binary). Modules form the internal structure within your crates.

The Road Ahead

In the next chapter, we'll delve into advanced module organization tactics, controlling visibility, and paths for ultimate project structuring flexibility.

Additional Resources

- **Modules in the Rust Book:**
  https://doc.rust-lang.org/book/ch07-00-modules.html
- **The use keyword:**
  https://doc.rust-lang.org/stable/rust-by-example/mod/use.html

_____

_____

_____

Mastering Modules: Advanced Tactics for Code Organization

In the previous chapter, we laid the foundation of Rust modules. Now, let's unlock more nuanced ways to manage code visibility, paths, and structure complex projects.

Controlling Visibility with pub

Fine-grained control over what's exposed outside a module is essential. Let's recap and expand:

- **pub:** Makes an item (struct, function, etc.) publicly accessible from outside the module.
- **(no keyword):** Default, the item is private within the module.
- **pub(crate):** The item is public within the current crate but not to external crates using your crate.
- **pub(in path):** Restricts visibility to a specific module subtree. Example: pub(in super::my_utilities)
- **pub(self):** The item is visible only within the current module.

Re-exporting: Sharing from Within a Module

Sometimes a module acts as a 'facade,' selectively re-exporting items from other modules it uses:

```
mod network {
    // ... networking module code ...
}


// Re-export a commonly used networking function.
pub use network::connect_to_server;
```

This simplifies usage for consumers of your crate.

Module Aliases: The as Keyword

If you have modules with long names or potential naming conflicts, use the as keyword to create aliases:

```
use super::long_module_name as concise_name;
```

Structuring Projects: Organizing Modules Across Files

As your project grows, consider these organization strategies:

- **File per Module:** Each module in its own file named after the module (e.g., `network.rs`).
- **Directories as Modules:** A directory containing a `mod.rs` file defines a module. Nested files/subdirectories can create a module hierarchy.

The Prelude: Automatically Imported Items

Rust has a special 'prelude' – a set of items brought into the scope of every module automatically. It includes common types like `Option`, `Result`, and `Vec`.

Tips

- **Start Simple:** Begin with simple module structures, refactoring as your project evolves.
- **Balance Granularity:** Avoid modules that are too small or too large. Find a good middle ground.
- **Namespace Wisely:** Choose descriptive names to prevent module naming conflicts.

Coming Up: Unraveling Types

Our next stop is a deep dive into Rust's type system. We'll explore scalar types, compound types, and the fundamentals of creating your own robust data structures.

Additional Resources

- **Rust by Example - Modules:**
  https://doc.rust-lang.org/rust-by-example/mod.html
- **Visibility and Privacy:**
  https://doc.rust-lang.org/book/ch07-02-defining-modules-to-control-scope-and-privacy.html

---

Section 2:
Conquering Types & Flow Control

Embracing Scalar Types: Foundations of Rust's Basic Data Entities

Scalar types, sometimes called primitive types, form the backbone of how we store and manipulate individual pieces of data in Rust programs. Let's dissect the key categories:

Numeric Types

- **Integers:** Represent whole numbers. Rust offers several integer types, each with varying size and signedness options:
  - **Signed:** Can be negative, zero, or positive (i8, i16, i32, i64, i128)
  - **Unsigned:** Only zero or positive. (u8, u16, u32, u64, u128)
- The number suffix indicates the size in bits they occupy in memory. i32 is generally the default if you don't have specific reasons to choose another.

- **Floating-Point:** Represent real numbers with decimal components. Rust primarily uses:
    - **f32:** Single-precision floating-point.
    - **f64:** Double-precision floating-point (the default for decimals).

Example

```
let score: i32 = 95;
let temperature: f64 = 37.8;
let initial: char = 'R';
let is_ready: bool = true;
```

Boolean (bool)

Represents logical values:

- **true**
- **false**

Mainly used within control-flow structures (like if, while).

Characters (char)

Rust's char type is powerful! It represents a single Unicode character, encompassing far more than just standard ASCII characters. You can store letters, numbers, emojis, and symbols from various languages.

```
let my_emoji = '🚀';
```

Choosing the Right Type

- **Precision vs. Memory:** Larger numeric types offer more range or precision but consume more memory.
- **Expected Values:** If you know a value will always be positive, an unsigned integer is fitting.
- **Performance:** While Rust is fast, smaller types can sometimes lead to marginally optimized computations.

Literals and Inference

Rust usually infers the type of a scalar value from how you initialize it. You can also be explicit:

```
let x = 10;      // Inferred as i32
let y: f64 = 3.14;
```

Type Conversions

You'll sometimes need to convert between scalar types. This can be done either:

- **Implicitly:** Rust might do this for you in specific scenarios where conversions are non-lossy.
- **Explicitly:** Use the as keyword for more control, specifying the target type: `let a = my_integer as f64`

Next Up: Advanced Type Insights

In the coming chapter, we'll delve into the nuances of scalar types, including their size limitations, how to perform operations on them, and potential gotchas to watch out for.

Additional Resources

- **Primitive Types in the Rust Book:** https://doc.rust-lang.org/book/ch03-02-data-types.html
- **Unicode Support:** https://www.unicode.org/

Unpacking Scalar Types: Advanced Insights into Rust's Core Data Structures

In the previous chapter, we introduced the basic scalar types. Now, let's go beyond the surface and uncover some important nuances.

Integer Size Limits

Each integer type has a finite range it can represent:

- **Example:** an i8 can store values from -128 to 127.
- Attempting to store a number outside this range can lead to **integer overflow**, a typical source of bugs.

Overflow Behavior

Rust's default behavior in debug mode is to panic (crash) if an overflow occurs. In release builds, it wraps around, potentially leading to unexpected results. You can perform explicit checked arithmetic with methods like checked_add, which return an Option to signal if an error occurred.

Floating-Point Trade-offs

Floating-point numbers introduce a different challenge:

- **Precision:** They can't represent all real numbers perfectly. Rounding errors are common, especially with repeated calculations.
- **Comparisons:** Avoid directly comparing floats with ==. Instead, check if the difference between floats falls within an acceptable tolerance.

Type Suffices

Sometimes you need more granularity in number representation than the standard types provide. Rust's numeric suffixes let you specify the exact size if needed:

```
let num_u8: u8 = 255u8;    // Explicitly an 8-bit
unsigned integer
```

```
let num_i16: i16 = -30000i16; // Explicitly a 16-bit
signed integer
```

Operators and Type Consistency

Rust is generally strict about types within mathematical operations. Let's see examples:

- **Mixing Integer Sizes:** `let result = x + y;` will fail if x is i32 and y is i16. You might need explicit conversions.
- **Division Quirks:** Integer division truncates. `5 / 2` results in 2, not `2.5`. Use floating-point types for decimal results where needed.

The Unicode Power of char

Remember, Rust's `char` is mighty! Here's why:

- **Size:** 4 bytes to represent a vast array of Unicode characters.
- **Emoji Support:** `let star = '🌟'`. Emojis are valid `char` values.
- **More Than Letters:** You can store Chinese characters, mathematical symbols, and more.

Beyond the Basics

We've only scratched the surface of the complexities surrounding scalar types!

- **Platform Considerations:** The exact size of types like `usize` and `isize` can vary slightly depending on the target architecture of your program (e.g., 32-bit vs. 64-bit systems).

Additional Resources

- **Numeric Types in Rust:** https://doc.rust-lang.org/book/ch03-02-data-types.html#numeric-types

- **Checked Arithmetic:**
  https://doc.rust-lang.org/book/ch03-02-data-types.html#integer-overflow
- **Floating-point Imprecision:** https://0.30000000000000004.com/

Next: Compound Types

Our next adventure is to dissect compound types, where we'll learn to build more complex data structures from these fundamental building blocks.

Decoding Compound Types: Exploring Rust's Complex Data Constructs

So far, we've worked with scalar types, each representing a single value. Compound types empower you to group multiple values of potentially different types into a cohesive unit. Let's explore Rust's primary compound types:

1. Tuples

- **Fixed-Size Collections:** Tuples hold an ordered sequence of elements. The elements can be of different types.
- **Defining Tuples:** `let coordinates = (30, 50, 2.5);`
- **Accessing Elements:** Use zero-based indexing or pattern matching:

```
let (x, y, z) = coordinates;
println!("X-Coordinate: {}", x);
```

Use Cases for Tuples

- Returning multiple values from a function.

- Representing data where the position of each element has meaning (like coordinates or RGB color values).

2. Arrays

- **Fixed-Size, Homogeneous:** Arrays store a collection of elements of the *same* type. The size of an array is determined at compile time.
- **Defining Arrays:** `let days_of_week = ["Mon", "Tue", "Wed", "Thu", "Fri", "Sat", "Sun"];`
- **Accessing Elements:** Zero-based indexing: `println!("First Day: {}", days_of_week[0]);`

Use Cases for Arrays

- Lists with a known, unchanging size.
- Performance-critical scenarios where fixed size offers a slight advantage.

3. Structs (We'll go in-depth in later chapters)

- **Custom Blueprints:** Structs let you define your own structured data types.
- **Example:**

```
struct Student {
    name: String,
    grade: u8,
    courses: Vec<String>
}
```

- **Creating Instances:** `let student1 = Student { name: "Alice".to_string(), grade: 11, courses: vec!["Math".to_string(), "Science".to_string()] };`
- **Accessing Fields:** Dot notation: `println!("Student Name: {}", student1.name);`

Use Cases for Structs

- The heart of most Rust programs.
- Modeling real-world entities with associated attributes and behaviors.

Choosing the Right Compound Type

- **Heterogeneity vs. Homogeneity:** Need elements of different types? Tuples. Fixed type? Arrays.
- **Meaningful Structure:** Want to name fields and group related data? Structs.
- **Size and Performance:** Arrays can have a slight performance edge for fixed-size scenarios.

Beyond the Basics

- **Nested Compound Types:** You can have structs containing arrays, tuples inside structs, and other combinations!
- **Memory Layout:** Understanding how compound types are arranged in memory is beneficial as you start to optimize Rust code.

Next: Mastering Compound Types

In the next chapter, we'll delve deeper into advanced techniques, including powerful ways to work with tuples, arrays, and the nuances of creating sophisticated custom structs.

Additional Resources

- **Rust documentation on Tuples:**
  https://doc.rust-lang.org/std/primitive.tuple.html
- **Rust Documentation on Arrays:**
  https://doc.rust-lang.org/std/primitive.array.html

Advancing with Compound Types: Mastering Advanced Data Structures in Rust

Tuple Power-Ups

While tuples might seem simple, there's more to them than meets the eye. Let's uncover some techniques:

Pattern Matching for Destructuring:

```
let student = ("Alice", 95, true);
let (name, _, is_passing) = student;  // Ignore the
score
```

-
- **The Unit Type (( )):** Sometimes, functions might not return a meaningful value. The unit type, represented by ( ), acts as a placeholder.
- **Tuples as Function Arguments:** They offer a concise way to pass multiple arguments to a function.

Array Mastery

Let's delve deeper into the realm of arrays:

- **Iteration:** `for item in my_array { ... }`
- **Slices:** Views into a portion of an array (more on these in later chapters). They are incredibly versatile.
- **Methods:** Arrays offer handy methods like:
    - `my_array.len()`: Length of the array
    - `my_array.contains(&value)`: Check if an element exists
    - `my_array.sort()`: Sort the elements

Tips:

- **Bounds Checking:** Rust performs bounds checks at runtime. Accessing an array element out of bounds will cause a panic.
- **Vectors for Flexibility:** If you need an array-like structure that can grow or shrink, Rust's Vec type is the solution (explored in later chapters).

Struct Superpowers

Structs are the cornerstone of modeling real-world concepts in Rust. Let's amplify your struct skills:

- **Tuple Structs:** These are like hybrid structs acting as named tuples. Useful for scenarios where you need the structure of a tuple but want more descriptive field names.

```
struct Color(u8, u8, u8); // RGB color
representation
```

- **Unit-like Structs:** Contain no fields. They primarily serve as custom type markers to enhance your code's meaning.
- **Struct Update Syntax:**

```
let student2 = Student { grade: 12, ..student1
};  // Update 'grade', keep other fields from
'student1'
```

Coming Up: Flow Control

With a strong grasp of compound types, we're ready to dive into the world of control flow – mechanisms to direct the execution path of your Rust programs based on conditions.

Additional Resources

- **Pattern Matching in Rust:** https://doc.rust-lang.org/book/ch18-00-patterns.html
- **Array Methods in the Rust Book:** https://doc.rust-lang.org/book/ch08-01-vectors.html#methods-on-arrays-and-slices

Orchestrating Control Flow: Directing Your Rust Code's Pathways

Beyond linear sequences of instructions, the essence of programming lies in decision-making and repetition. Rust provides a rich set of tools to control the flow of your code's logic.

Conditional Execution: `if` and `else`

- **Decisions, Decisions:** `if` statements let your code execute different blocks based on Boolean conditions:

```rust
let age = 25;

if age >= 21 {
    println!("You can purchase that beverage!");
} else {
    println!("Sorry, you're not old enough yet.");
}
```

- **Chain of Alternatives:** `else if` for multiple possibilities:

```rust
let score = 85;

if score >= 90 {
    println!("Excellent! Grade: A");
} else if score >= 80 {
    println!("Good Work! Grade: B");
} else {
    println!("Let's aim higher next time.");
}
```

Controlling Repetition: Loops

Rust offers several looping mechanisms for when you need to repeat actions:

- **loop:** The most basic - repeats indefinitely until you explicitly break out of it using the `break` keyword.

```
loop {
    println!("This will repeat forever (unless
we use 'break')");
}
```

- **while:** Repeats a block while a condition remains true:

```
let mut counter = 3;
while counter > 0 {
    println!("Countdown: {}", counter);
    counter -= 1;
}
println!("Blast Off!");
```

- **for:** Ideal for iterating over sequences (like arrays, ranges, or collections that we'll introduce later):

```
let numbers = [10, 20, 30];
for number in numbers.iter() {
    println!("Doubled: {}", number * 2);
}
```

The Power of Pattern Matching: match

Rust's `match` expression is like a supercharged `switch` statement from other languages, allowing for elegant and expressive control flow.

```
let grade_level = 10;
```

```
match grade_level {
    9 ... 12 => println!("High School"),
    6 ... 8 => println!("Middle School"),
    _ => println!("Elementary School or other")
// Catch-all case
}
```

Tips

- **Indentation Matters:** Rust uses curly braces { } and indentation to signify blocks of code associated with conditional branches or loops.
- **Early Exits:** Use `break` to exit a loop prematurely and `continue` to skip to the next iteration.
- **Choose Wisely:** `if` expressions are for branching, loops are for repetition. Select the right tool for the task.

Next: Refining Control Flow

In the next chapter, we'll go deeper, exploring techniques to make your control flow structures more concise, handle errors gracefully, and uncover advanced pattern-matching capabilities in Rust.

Additional Resources

- **Rust's Control Flow Documentation:**
  https://doc.rust-lang.org/book/ch03-05-control-flow.html
- **The `match` statement:**
  https://doc.rust-lang.org/book/ch06-02-match.html

Fine-Tuning Control Flow: Advanced Strategies for Flow Control Mastery

Concise Conditional Expressions

Rust allows if and else to be used as expressions, assigning a value directly:

```
let is_ready = if age >= 18 { true } else { false };

let discount = if customer_status == "VIP" { 0.25 } else { 0.1 };
```

Loop Labels: Breaking Out of Nested Loops

Sometimes, you need more control over breaking out of multiple nested loops. Loop labels to the rescue!

```
'outer_loop: for x in 0..5 {
  for y in 0..5 {
      if x * y > 20 {
          break 'outer_loop; // Breaks out of the outermost loop
      }
  }
}
```

Mastering match Patterns

Rust's match goes beyond simple comparisons. Let's explore its prowess:

- **Ranges:** `1...10 => println!("Within the first ten")`
- **Guards:** `Some(x) if x % 2 == 0 => println!("Even number within Option")`
- **Destructuring:** `Point { x, y } => println!("Coordinates: ({}, {})", x, y)` (More on structs later!)

Error Handling with Result

The `Result` type (an enum we'll look at closely later) is crucial for graceful error handling in Rust:

```rust
fn divide(a: i32, b: i32) -> Result<i32, String> {
    if b == 0 {
        Err("Division by zero!".to_string())
    } else {
        Ok(a / b)
    }
}
```

Let the caller of `divide` handle the potential error using `match` or other Result methods.

The ? Operator: Error Shortcutting

For streamlined error propagation, the ? operator offers a shortcut within functions that return `Result`.

```rust
fn open_file(filename: &str) -> Result<String,
std::io::Error> {
    let mut file = std::fs::File::open(filename)?;
    let mut contents = String::new();
    file.read_to_string(&mut contents)?;
    Ok(contents)
}
```

Loops as Expressions

Loops in Rust can sometimes produce values:

- **break with a value:** Break out of a loop and return that value. Perfect for search scenarios like finding an element in a list.

Up Ahead: Text & Collections

Our next adventure will be unraveling `String`, Rust's way of handling text, and the techniques for manipulating textual data. Then, we'll look at powerful collections that let you store and organize multiple values.

Additional Resources

- **Loop Labels:**
  https://doc.rust-lang.org/book/ch03-05-control-flow.html#loop-labels
- **Match Patterns:**
  https://doc.rust-lang.org/book/ch06-02-match.html#match-patterns
- **The Rust Result Type** https://doc.rust-lang.org/std/result/
- **The Question Mark Operator:**
  https://doc.rust-lang.org/book/ch09-02-recoverable-errors-with-result.html#propagating-errors

---

Unraveling Strings: Understanding Rust's Textual Data Handling

In many languages, strings seem deceptively simple. Rust delves deeper, providing both power and a layer of safety when working with textual data.

Two Faces of Strings

1. `String`: A growable, owned, UTF-8 encoded text data type.
- You can create, modify, and manipulate `String` objects.
- Example: `let mut greeting = String::from("Hello");`
2. **&str (string slice):** A reference (a 'view') into a portion of a string.
- Immutable by default. Think of it like a pointer to some string data, often within a `String` or even hardcoded into your program.
- Example: `let name = &greeting[0..5]; // name is a &str containing "Hello"`

Key Points About Rust Strings

- **UTF-8 by Default:** Rust's commitment to Unicode means you can store characters from various languages out of the box.
- **No "Raw" String Literals:** Unlike some languages, every string literal in Rust is already a UTF-8 encoded &str.
- **Ownership:** String takes ownership of the text data, making it responsible for managing memory.
- **Immutability of &str:** String slices themselves are immutable. To modify, you usually need to work with a String.

UTF-8: The Universal Text Format

Rust's dedication to UTF-8 encoding means your String objects can hold text from almost any language, emojis, and a wide array of symbols. However, this makes some operations more complex:

- **Length is NOT Bytes:** greeting.len() might be different from greeting.as_bytes().len(). A single character could take multiple bytes!
- **Indexing is Tricky:** You can't directly access a character by index like greeting[1]. UTF-8 characters have variable widths.

String Creation

Several ways to bring a String into existence:

```
let greeting = "Hello".to_string(); // From a string
literal

let mut farewell = String::new(); // Start with an
empty String
farewell.push_str("Goodbye!");

let composed = format!("{}, {}", greeting,
farewell); // Formatting magic!
```

Many ways to build strings exist:

- **Literals:** `"This is a string literal"` (This is usually a `&str`).
- **`String::new()`:** Starts with an empty string.
- **`String::from("Text")`:** Common way to convert a `&str` to a `String`.
- **`format!` Macro:** Powerful tool to build complex strings: `let message = format!("{}/{}", score, total);`

Slicing and Dicing (&str)

Extract substrings without making full copies:

```rust
let name = "Ferris the Crab";
let first_name = &name[0..6];   // "Ferris"
```

Caution! Rust checks UTF-8 boundaries at compile-time, preventing you from accidentally slicing in the middle of a multi-byte character.

Iterating over Characters

There are a few ways to handle the complexities of Unicode:

- **`.chars()`:** Iterates over individual Unicode characters.
- **`.bytes()`:** If you need access to the raw bytes making up the UTF-8 encoding.

Modifying Strings

`String` offers a host of methods for modifications:

```rust
let mut tagline = String::from("Rust: Empowering Everyone");
tagline.push('!'); // Add a single character
tagline.remove(5);   // Remove by index
tagline.replace("Everyone", "Developers");
```

A Note on Performance

If you're doing heavily text manipulation, understand that creating and modifying Strings can cause memory reallocations. Sometimes other strategies might be more efficient for specific scenarios.

Manipulating Strings

Rust gives you a rich toolkit (we'll explore more in the next chapter):

- **Concatenation:** `push_str` to append to a `String`, or the + operator (which takes ownership for String + &str).
- **Iterating:** `for char in message.chars() { ... }` Note: iterates over Unicode characters.

`String` vs. `&str` : When to Choose

- **Need Ownership?** Modifying, growing, or taking ownership of the text requires a `String`.
- **Read-Only, Short-Lived Reference?** A `&str` is efficient and avoids unnecessary copies.
- **Function Parameters:** Often, accepting a `&str` makes your functions more flexible!

String Internals (A Peek)

Behind the scenes, a `String` is essentially a vector of bytes (like an array) ensuring UTF-8 validity, plus metadata about its capacity. This is why it can grow and shrink.

Ahead! String Mastery

Next, let's learn how to slice, dice, search, transform, and master the manipulation of text data within Rust.

Additional Resources

- **Rust Strings in the Book:** https://doc.rust-lang.org/book/ch08-02-strings.html
- **The format! Macro:** https://doc.rust-lang.org/std/fmt/
- **UTF-8 Background:** https://en.wikipedia.org/wiki/UTF-8

- **Unicode:** https://www.unicode.org/

_____

_____

_____

String Manipulation Mastery: Advanced Techniques for String Processing in Rust

Common String Transformations

- **Changing Case:**

```
let message = "rUsT iS fUn!";
println!("Lowercase: {}",
message.to_lowercase());
 println!("Uppercase: {}",
message.to_uppercase());
```

- **Trimming Whitespace:**

```
let padded = "   Hello, World!   ";
println!("Trimmed: {}", padded.trim());
```

- **Splitting and Joining:**

```
let words = "one,two,three";
let word_vec: Vec<&str> =
words.split(',').collect(); // Split into a
vector

let sentence = word_vec.join(" "); // Rejoin
with spaces
```

Search and Replace

- **Finding Substrings:**

```
let text = "The quick brown fox";
if text.contains("quick") {
    println!("Found 'quick'!");
}
```

- **Replacing Patterns:**

```
let updated = text.replace("brown", "rusty");
```

Regular Expressions (A Powerful Tool)

For complex pattern matching, Rust has the `regex` crate (we'd need to add it as a Cargo dependency):

```
use regex::Regex;

let email_pattern =
Regex::new(r"^([a-z0-9_.-]+)@([\da-z.-]+)\.([a-z
.]{2,6})$").unwrap();

if email_pattern.is_match("test@example.com") {
    println!("Valid email");
}
```

Beyond the Basics

- **Performance Considerations:** Heavy string manipulation can sometimes create many intermediate `String`s. Understanding memory implications is vital for optimization.
- **Internationalization:** Rust provides libraries to help if you need to work with text in different languages and character sets properly.

String Formatting on Steroids

Recall the `format!` macro – it's even more potent than you might realize:

```
let item = "apple";
let price = 2.5;
let formatted_string = format!("You bought a {} for
${:.2}", item, price);
// Output: "You bought a apple for $2.50"
```

Next Up: Mastering Ownership

We're about to venture into the heart of Rust – ownership, borrowing, and lifetimes. Understanding these concepts is vital for building safe and efficient Rust programs!

Additional Resources

- **Rust's String API:**
  https://doc.rust-lang.org/std/string/struct.String.html
- **The Regex Crate:** https://crates.io/crates/regex
- **The format! macro:** https://doc.rust-lang.org/std/fmt/

Section 3:
Mastering Rust's Core Concepts

Embracing Ownership: The Foundation of Rust's Unique Paradigm

The Core Idea: Every Value Has a Single Owner

At any given time in your Rust program, each value has one variable that is its owner. Here's why this matters tremendously:

1. **Memory Safety:** When the owner goes out of scope, the value's memory is automatically cleaned up (*dropped*). No dangling pointers, no memory leaks!
2. **No Garbage Collection Pauses:** Rust determines cleanup deterministically at compile time, not at unpredictable intervals during your program's execution.

Ownership Rules

1. **Each value has ONE owner.**
2. **When the owner goes out of scope, the value is dropped.**
3. **Ownership can be transferred (moved).**
4. **You can temporarily borrow values with references.**

Example: Moving Ownership

```rust
let msg1 = String::from("Greetings"); // msg1 owns
the String data
let msg2 = msg1; // Ownership *moved* to msg2, msg1
is invalid now

// println!(msg1); // Error: msg1 no longer valid
println!("{}", msg2);
```

Copying vs. Moving

- **Scalar Types:** Values generally get copied (integers, floats, booleans, etc.). These types usually have a known, fixed size and are cheap to copy.
- **Heap-Allocated Data:** Data like `String` or custom structs involve heap allocation. Copies would be expensive, so ownership *moves* by default.

Functions and Ownership

- **Taking Ownership:** A function taking ownership of an argument becomes its new owner.

```rust
fn print_message(msg: String) {
```

```
        println!("Your message: {}", msg);
} // msg is dropped here
```

- **Returning Ownership:** You can return ownership back from a function:

```
fn generate_greeting() -> String {
    String::from("Hello")
} // Ownership of the String is transferred to
the caller
```

Additional Resources

- **Ownership in the Rust Book:**
  https://doc.rust-lang.org/book/ch04-01-what-is-ownership.html

Tip: Experiment with small Rust examples to visualize how ownership gets transferred. Misunderstandings early on will lead to fighting the compiler – getting ownership right will make the compiler your ally.

Empowering Ownership: Advanced Strategies for Memory Management in Rust

In the previous chapter, we laid the foundation of ownership. Now, let's explore techniques to use it to our advantage while overcoming potential limitations.

When Copying *Is* the Answer

Sometimes, you truly need a full copy of data. Rust lets you copy certain types using the clone method:

```
let num = 10;
let num_copy = num.clone(); // Explicit copy of an
integer

let message = String::from("Hello");
let another_message = message.clone(); // May be
more expensive due to heap data
```

Important: Types must implement the `Clone` trait to be cloneable.

Partial Copies with Rc

What if you want multiple owners of the same data on the heap in a limited way? Rc (Reference Counted) to the rescue!

```
use std::rc::Rc;

let message = Rc::new(String::from("Hello there!"));
let message2 = Rc::clone(&message); // 'message' and
'message2' share ownership
```

- **Use Cases:** When you require multiple handles to the same data without worrying about the intricate details of borrowing.
- **Trade-off:** Rc has some runtime overhead to track the reference count.

Cell Types: Interior Mutability

Sometimes, you need to modify a value even when you technically don't own it due to Rust's immutability rules. Cell types help!

- **Cell<T>:** Allows setting/getting the inner value, even from a reference.
- **RefCell<T>:** Enforces Rust's borrowing rules at runtime (you can get mutable references for short intervals), potentially causing panics if you violate the rules.

Use Cases:

- Modifying a piece of data within a struct from multiple locations.

- Situations where compile-time borrow checking gets too restrictive.

Caution: Cell types can make your Rust code less provably safe as they bend the core rules.

Ownership, Performance, and Clarity

Rust's ownership model guides you towards safe and often performant code. Consider these points:

- **Prefer default ownership semantics.** Start by transferring values and letting Rust clean them up for you.
- **Be mindful of copies.** Understand when data is copied vs. moved.
- **Reach for advanced tools strategically.** Don't default to `clone`, Rc, or cell types without good reason.

Next Up: References & Borrowing

The key to flexibility within Rust's ownership model lies in references and borrowing. Let's dive into the powerful world of safely sharing data without transferring ownership.

Additional Resources

- **The `clone` method:**
  https://doc.rust-lang.org/std/clone/trait.Clone.html
- **Rc (Reference Counted) type:**
  https://doc.rust-lang.org/std/rc/struct.Rc.html
- **Cell and RefCell:** https://doc.rust-lang.org/std/cell/

Navigating References & Borrowing: Unlocking Rust's Key Sharing Mechanisms

Think of references as temporary, read-only (sometimes writable!) pointers to data owned by something else. The magic comes from Rust's rules that the compiler enforces to prevent data races and memory issues.

Introducing the &

You create references using the ampersand operator &:

```
let number = 42;
let number_ref = &number;  // `number_ref` is a
reference to `number`

println!("Value through reference: {}", number_ref);
```

Key Rules of Borrowing

1. **At any given time, you can have either:**
   - One mutable reference (&mut) **OR**
   - Any number of immutable references (&)
2. **References must be valid:** You can't have a reference pointing to data that's gone out of scope and been cleaned up.

Why Borrowing Matters

- **Efficiency:** Passing references avoids copying large amounts of data.
- **Flexibility:** Allow multiple parts of your code to access data without transferring ownership.
- **Safety:** Rust's compile-time borrow checker eliminates a whole class of potential bugs!

Example: Iterating over Items

```
let numbers = vec![1, 2, 3];
```

```
for num in &numbers {   // Use a reference to avoid
consuming the vector
    println!("{}", num);
}
```

Mutable Borrows (&mut)

```
let mut count = 0;
increment(&mut count); // Mutable borrow to modify
'count'

fn increment(num: &mut i32) {
    *num += 1; // Dereferencing to change the value
}
```

Common Pitfalls

- **Fighting the Borrow Checker:** Initially, the compiler's restrictions might feel like roadblocks. Persistence pays off – the compiler is pushing you towards safer code.
- **Overusing Copies:** Don't default to clone unnecessarily, as references often enable better performance.

Lifetimes (A Taste of Things to Come)

Rust has a sophisticated system (*lifetimes*) to track how long references remain valid. This helps prevent dangling pointers. We'll explore lifetimes more in later chapters!

Next: Mastering References

In the upcoming chapter, we'll delve into practical scenarios and advanced reference usage techniques to solidify your grasp of this core Rust concept.

Additional Resources

- **References and Borrowing in the Rust Book:**
  https://doc.rust-lang.org/book/ch04-02-references-and-borrowing.html

Tip: Try writing small code snippets that purposely violate borrowing rules and observe the compiler's error messages. This is a great way to understand the restrictions better.

Maximizing References & Borrowing: Advanced Techniques for Resource Management in Rust

References to Struct Fields

You can borrow individual fields of a struct, enabling granular control:

```rust
struct Player {
    name: String,
    score: i32,
}

let mut player = Player { name: "Alice".to_string(),
score: 0 };

let name_ref = &player.name;
 &mut player.score += 10; // Mutable borrow for just
the 'score' field
```

Temporary Borrowing within Expressions

Sometimes, you need a short-term reference within an expression:

```rust
fn max_value(x: &i32, y: &i32) -> &i32 {
```

```
    if x > y { x } else { y }    // Returns a
reference
}
```

Controlling Behavior with References

Methods often take &self or &mut self, allowing you to dictate if the method can modify the object:

```
struct Counter {
    count: u32
}

impl Counter {
    fn increment(&mut self) {
        self.count += 1;
    }

    fn get_count(&self) -> u32 {
        self.count
    }
}
```

Slices: References to Portions

Slices (&[T]) are references to parts of arrays or vectors:

```
let arr = [5, 10, 15];
let middle = &arr[1..]; // Slice containing [10, 15]
```

Use Cases & Benefits

- **Network Sockets:** Borrow a socket to read/write data without transferring ownership.
- **File Handles:** Share a file handle for reading across different parts of your code.
- **Iterators:** Borrowing from collections allows for efficient chaining of operations.

The NLL (Non-Lexical Lifetimes)

Modern Rust has made borrow checking less strict due to NLL. The compiler often infers lifetimes correctly, but it's still essential to understand the underlying principles.

Tips

- **Start with Immutability:** If possible, use & references, upgrading to &mut only when necessary.
- **Consider Lifetimes:** Think about how long the references you create need to be valid.
- **Embrace the Compiler:** If the code doesn't compile, understand the borrowing errors and refactor, rather than reaching for clone too quickly.

The Road Ahead: Structs, Enums, and Beyond

We're about to embark on defining our own structs, which combined with references and borrowing, unlocks Rust's true power for data modeling. Then, we'll explore enums to enhance data representation!

Additional Resources

- **Slices in the Rust Book:**
  https://doc.rust-lang.org/book/ch04-03-slices.html
- **Non-Lexical Lifetimes:**
  https://doc.rust-lang.org/book/ch10-03-lifetime-syntax.html#lifetime-elision

Section 4:
Crafting Rust's Essential Components

Architecting Structs: Building Blocks of Rust's Data Organization

What is a Struct?

Think of a struct as a custom blueprint. It defines the fields (pieces of data) that a particular type of thing will hold. Here's a simple example:

```rust
struct User {
    username: String,
    email: String,
    active: bool,
}
```

Instantiating Structs

Once defined, you can create instances of your struct:

```rust
let user1 = User {
    username: "johndoe".to_string(),
    email: "john@example.com".to_string(),
    active: true,
};
```

Accessing Fields (Dot Notation)

Use the dot . operator to access individual fields of a struct instance:

```rust
println!("User email: {}", user1.email);
user1.active = false; // Modify a field
```

Struct Update Syntax

This concise syntax lets you create a new struct instance modifying a few fields of an existing one:

```rust
let updated_user = User {
```

```
    email: "jane@example.com".to_string(),
    ..user1 // ... brings in all other fields from
'user1'
};
```

Tuple Structs

These act like named tuples, mainly for concise data grouping:

```
struct Color(u8, u8, u8); // Represents an RGB color

let black = Color(0, 0, 0);
```

Unit-Like Structs

Structs with no fields. They act like markers or distinct identifiers:

```
struct LogEntry; // Could represent a log entry
event
```

Methods on Structs

You can associate functions with your structs using the `impl` keyword, allowing behavior connected to the data.

```
impl User {
    fn get_status(&self) -> String {
        if self.active {
            "Active".to_string()
        } else {
            "Inactive".to_string()
        }
    }
}

println!("{}", user1.get_status());
```

Let's Get Practical!

In the next chapter, we'll upgrade our skills by exploring more advanced struct techniques, including nesting structs to model complex relationships.

Additional Resources

- **Structs in the Rust Book:**
  https://doc.rust-lang.org/book/ch05-01-defining-structs.html

---

Advancing with Structs: Mastering Advanced Data Structures in Rust

Ownership within Structs

Fields of a struct can own their data, just like regular variables:

```rust
struct Task {
    description: String,
    completed: bool,
}
```

References Inside Structs

Sometimes you might want a struct field to be a reference, creating links between data:

```rust
struct Project {
    name: String,
    tasks: Vec<&Task> // A vector of references to
Tasks
}
```

Caution: Remember borrowing rules! The references inside a `Project` must not outlive the `Task` instances they point to.

Nested Structs: Building Relationships

Structs can contain other structs, creating hierarchical data models:

```
struct Employee {
    name: String,
    department: Department,
}

struct Department {
    name: String,
    location: String,
}
```

Struct Methods: Beyond Simple Data

Let's revisit methods on structs to focus on some more advanced uses:

- **Constructors:** Often helpful to use a function rather than direct field assignment.

  ```
  impl Task {
      fn new(desc: String) -> Task {
          Task {
              description: desc,
              completed: false
          }
      }
  }

  let task1 = Task::new("Write Rust book chapter".to_string());
  ```

- **Associated Functions:** Functions *associated* with a struct, but not tied to a specific instance (often used for creation or as utilities). They use `::` syntax instead of `.`

Derived Traits

Rust can automatically implement certain traits for your structs if their internal fields also implement those traits. Some common ones:

- **Debug:** Allows you to print structs with {:?} formatting for debugging.
- **Clone:** Necessary if you want to create full copies of structs.
- **PartialEq:** Enables comparing instances of your struct using ==.

Next: Traits – The Key to Abstraction

Our next adventure delves into traits – powerful tools for defining shared behaviors across different types in Rust, enabling both code reuse and flexibility.

Additional Resources

- **Nested Structs:**
  https://doc.rust-lang.org/book/ch05-01-defining-structs.html#using-structs-to-structure-related-data
- **Deriving Traits:**
  https://doc.rust-lang.org/book/ch10-02-traits.html#derivable-trait

_____

_____

_____

Unveiling Traits: Understanding Rust's Powerful Abstraction Mechanisms

What are Traits?

Think of traits as blueprints for shared behaviors. They define methods that a type must implement to be considered as having that trait. Let's see a simple example:

```
trait Report {
    fn generate_summary(&self) -> String;
```

```
}
```

Implementing Traits for Structs

You use the `impl` keyword to implement a trait for your custom struct:

```rust
struct NewsArticle {
    headline: String,
    content: String,
}

impl Report for NewsArticle {
    fn generate_summary(&self) -> String {
        format!("{} - {}", self.headline,
self.content[..100].to_string())
    }
}
```

Power #1: Generic Functions

Traits enable us to write functions that can work with diverse types, as long as they implement the required trait:

```rust
fn summarize_item<T: Report>(item: &T) {
    println!("Summary: {}",
item.generate_summary());
}
```

You can call `summarize_item` with any type that implements the `Report` trait!

Power #2: Trait Bounds

The `<T: Report>` syntax is called a trait bound. It specifies a constraint on the generic type T.

Default Implementations

Traits can provide default method implementations, which types can opt to override:

```
trait HasArea {
    fn area(&self) -> f64;

    fn is_larger_than(&self, other: &Self) -> bool {
// Default implementation
        self.area() > other.area()
    }
}
```

Common Built-in Traits

Rust's standard library has a treasure trove of useful traits:

- **Display:** For a string representation (like `println!` uses).
- **Debug:** For debugging output (`{:?}`).
- **Iterator:** For sequences that can be iterated over.
- **Clone:** For making copies.
- **And many more!**

Traits as Interfaces

Think of traits like interfaces in other languages. They define a contract that types must adhere to.

The Path Ahead: Maximizing Traits

Next, we'll look at maximizing the potential of traits, including using them with generics, advanced trait techniques, and designing your programs around traits for flexibility.

Additional Resources

- **Traits in the Rust Book:**
  https://doc.rust-lang.org/book/ch10-02-traits.html

Maximizing Traits: Advanced Strategies for Code Reusability in Rust

Traits and Generics – A Perfect Combo

Remember our `summarize_item` function from the previous chapter? Let's make it even more adaptable.

```rust
fn summarize<T>(item: &T) where T: Report + Display
{
    println!("Summary: {}",
item.generate_summary());
    println!("Item details: {}", item); // We can
use Display now!
}
```

Note the `where` clause – this specifies multiple trait bounds for our generic type T.

Trait Objects

To use traits for dynamic behavior where the concrete type might not be known at compile time, you need trait objects:

```rust
trait Shape {
    fn area(&self) -> f64;
}

struct Circle { radius: f64 }
 struct Rectangle { width: f64, height: f64 }

// ... (Implementations of the 'Shape' trait for
'Circle' and 'Rectangle')
```

```
fn get_shape() -> Box<dyn Shape> { // Using 'dyn'
for dynamic dispatch
    if get_random_boolean() {   // Some random
condition
        Box::new(Circle { radius: 5.0 })
    } else {
        Box::new(Rectangle { width: 10.0, height: 5.0
})
    }
}
```

```
let shape = get_shape();
println!("Area is: {}", shape.area());
```

Trait objects are akin to type-erased references. There's a slight performance trade-off due to dynamic dispatch (virtual method calls).

Static vs. Dynamic Dispatch

- **Generics with trait bounds:** Static dispatch, the compiler knows the concrete types at compile time. Generally faster.
- **Trait Objects (dyn Trait):** Dynamic dispatch, the concrete type is determined at runtime. Provides more flexibility at the cost of some overhead.

Operator Overloading with Traits

Rust lets you overload operators like +, -, *, allowing for custom behavior on your types using traits such as std::ops::Add:

```
use std::ops::Add;
```

```
impl Add for Point {
    type Output = Point;

    fn add(self, other: Point) -> Point { ... }
}
```

Marker Traits

These are traits with no methods, used just to tag types as having a certain property:

- **Copy:** Type can be copied with a simple bitwise copy.
- **Send:** Type is safe to transfer between threads.
- **Sync:** Type can be safely shared between threads (&T is safe).

Next Up: Collections

Rust has powerful collections like Vec, HashMap, and more. We'll see how these leverage traits and how you can make your own custom collections!

Additional Resources

- **Trait Objects**
  https://doc.rust-lang.org/book/ch17-02-trait-objects.html
- **Operator Overloading in Rust**
  https://doc.rust-lang.org/book/ch10-02-traits.html#operator-overloading-and-Default-Generic-Implementations
- **Marker Traits** https://doc.rust-lang.org/std/marker/

Harnessing Collections: Unleashing Rust's Data Storage Arsenal

Vec: The Versatile Workhorse

Vec<T>, the dynamic array, is likely your most-used collection. Let's recap and add some more skills:

- **Creating:** `let numbers = vec![1, 2, 3];`
- **Adding:** `numbers.push(4);`
- **Iterating:** `for num in &numbers { ... }`

- **Removing (Careful!)** Options include pop (from the end), or removing by index with remove (this can cause shifts within the Vec).

HashMap<K, V>: The Speedy Lookup Table

Hash maps excel at fast lookups using a key:

```
use std::collections::HashMap;
```

```
let mut scores = HashMap::new();
scores.insert("Player 1", 25);
 println!("Player 1 score: {:?}", scores.get("Player
1"));
```

- **Important:** Keys must implement the Eq and Hash traits.
- **Tip:** Choose HashMap when you primarily need fast access to values by a key.

BTreeSet and BTreeMap<K, V>: Keep Things Sorted

BTreeSet and BTreeMap maintain the order of their elements:

```
use std::collections::BTreeSet;
```

```
let mut unique_numbers = BTreeSet::new();
unique_numbers.insert(5);
unique_numbers.insert(5); // Will insert only once
since it's a set
```

- **Use Cases:** When the order of elements is important or you need to eliminate duplicates.

The Power of Collection Methods

Iterators (which we'll explore further when we cover closures) and collections go hand-in-hand. Common ones to know:

- **iter():** Gives an immutable iterator over a collection.
- **iter_mut():** Gives a mutable iterator.

- `into_iter()`: Consumes the collection and gives ownership of the items.
- **map, filter, fold/reduce, and many more!**

Collection Tips

- **Choosing the Right Tool:** Consider how you'll be accessing the data (sequential, by key, ordering important?)
- **Be Mindful of Performance:** Some operations, like inserting into the middle of a `Vec`, can be more expensive than others.
- **Traits Matter:** Many collection operations are powered by traits like `Iterator`.

Up Next: Mastering Collection Efficiency

In the next chapter, we'll delve into performance considerations, choosing the correct collection based on your use cases, and optimizing your code for working with collections effectively.

Additional Resources

- **Vec:** https://doc.rust-lang.org/std/vec/struct.Vec.html
- **HashMap:** https://doc.rust-lang.org/std/collections/struct.HashMap.html
- **BTreeSet / BTreeMap:** https://doc.rust-lang.org/std/collections/

Optimizing Collections: Advanced Techniques for Data Handling in Rust

Pre-allocating Vec Capacity

If you have a good idea of how big a `Vec` needs to be, preallocate space:

```
let mut numbers = Vec::with_capacity(100); //
Reserves space for 100 elements
for i in 0..100 {
    numbers.push(i); // No reallocations likely
needed
}
```

Choosing the Right Hashmap Implementation

The default hasher in Rust is usually good, but if performance is critical consider alternatives:

- `fxhash` (often faster, but potential security risks in certain network situations)
- `fnv`
- **Custom hash implementations if you have a very specific use-case**

Understand Iterator Costs

While incredibly powerful, iterator chains can sometimes have hidden costs. Know your methods:

- `map`, `filter`: Generally fast and lazy.
- `collect()`: Materializes an entire new collection which can be expensive for large datasets.

Sorting Strategies

Choose your sorting algorithm wisely:

- `sort()`: Rust's default is a stable (preserves the order of equal elements) hybrid sorting algorithm – good for most cases.
- `sort_unstable()`: Can be faster if you don't care about stability.
- **Specialized sorts:** Check if your data's properties allow for more efficient sorting (e.g., already partially ordered)

Beyond the Basics

- **Entry API:** For efficient in-place modifications or checking if a key exists in a `HashMap`.
- **Shrinking to Fit:** Use `Vec::shrink_to_fit()` to free up excess capacity after insertions.
- **Custom Collections:** For highly specialized needs, you might even build your own collection types, although this is less common.

Profiling Is Key

When optimizing, use a profiler (even simple ones built into tools like Cargo) to identify the true bottlenecks in your program. Don't optimize prematurely!

The Road Ahead: Versatile Data Enumeration

Next up, we introduce enums – a powerful Rust construct for modeling data that can take on one of several distinct variants, enhancing your code's expressiveness and safety.

Additional Resources

- **Choosing a Hash Function:**
  https://doc.rust-lang.org/std/hash/index.html
- **The Entry API:**
  https://doc.rust-lang.org/std/collections/hash_map/enum.Entry.html

Tip: Experiment! Create benchmarks to compare the impact of different collection choices and techniques on your specific use cases.

Deciphering Enums: Understanding Rust's Versatile Data Enumeration

Enums 101

Let's imagine we're modeling playing card suits:

```rust
enum Suit {
    Hearts,
    Diamonds,
    Clubs,
    Spades
}
```

- Each variant (Hearts, Diamonds, etc.) is like a unique value the Suit type can hold.

Using Enums

```rust
let card_suit = Suit::Clubs;

match card_suit {  // Pattern matching against the enum variants
    Suit::Hearts => println!("The suit is Hearts"),
    Suit::Diamonds => println!("The suit is Diamonds"),
    // ...and so on
}
```

Enums with Data

Enums become even more powerful when their variants carry associated data:

```rust
enum PaymentStatus {
    Paid(String), // Holds a transaction ID
    Pending,
    Refunded(f64) // Holds the refund amount
```

```
}
```

The Power of `match`

Rust's `match` expression shines with enums, letting you write logic for each variant:

```
let status = PaymentStatus::Pending;

match status {
    PaymentStatus::Paid(id) => println!("Paid!
Transaction ID: {}", id),
    PaymentStatus::Pending => println!("Awaiting
payment..."),
    PaymentStatus::Refunded(amount) =>
println!("Refund issued: {}", amount),
}
```

Enums vs. Structs

- **Enums:** Represent one of several possibilities.
- **Structs:** Group multiple pieces of related data together.

Enums in Practice

- **Option:** The core Rust enum! Some(T) represents a value, None represents its absence.
- **Result<T, E>:** For error handling! Ok(T) for success, Err(E) for failure.
- **State Machines:** Enums model the different states of a system.
- **Network Protocols:** Different packet types can be represented as enum variants.

Advancing with Enums: Mastering Complex Data Enumeration in Rust

Methods on Enums

Just as structs can have methods, enums can too! Let's enhance our PaymentStatus:

```rust
enum PaymentStatus {
    Paid(String),
    Pending,
    Refunded(f64)
}

impl PaymentStatus {
    fn display_status(&self) -> String {
        match self {
            PaymentStatus::Paid(ref id) =>
format!("Paid (ID: {})", id),
            PaymentStatus::Pending => "Payment in
progress".to_string(),
            PaymentStatus::Refunded(amount) =>
format!("Refunded: ${:.2}", amount),
        }
    }
}
```

Now we can do: `println!("{}",
PaymentStatus::Paid("12345".to_string()).display_stat
us())`

Enums and Traits

Let's say we want all our different card suits to be displayable:

```rust
enum Suit { ... } // Our Suit enum from earlier
```

```
impl std::fmt::Display for Suit {
    fn fmt(&self, f: &mut std::fmt::Formatter<'_>)
-> std::fmt::Result {
        match self {
            Suit::Hearts   => write!(f, "♥"),
            Suit::Diamonds => write!(f, "♦"),
            // ... rest of the suits
        }
    }
}
```

The 'C-like' Advantage

Rust enums can sometimes closely mimic their C counterparts. Each variant can be assigned a numeric discriminant:

```
enum ErrorCode {
    FileNotFound = 1,
    InvalidPermissions = 2,
    // ...and so on
}
```

'if let' for Convenient Matching

Sometimes you need to handle only a specific variant:

```
let status = PaymentStatus::Pending;

if let PaymentStatus::Pending = status {
    println!("Waiting for payment to complete...");
}
```

Enums as Control Flow Tools

Enums are perfect for modeling state machines and workflows where your data can be in one of a finite number of distinct states.

Up Next: Functional Power with Closures

We're heading into Rust's functional side. Learn how closures let you treat code as data, enabling elegant patterns like filtering and mapping collections.

Additional Resources

- **Methods on Enums:**
  https://doc.rust-lang.org/book/ch06-02-match.html#methods
- **'if let' in Rust:** https://doc.rust-lang.org/book/ch06-03-if-let.html

---

Embracing Closures: Harnessing Rust's Functional Power

What are Closures?

Think of closures as anonymous functions that can capture variables from their surrounding environment. Here's a simple example:

```
let add_five = |num: i32| num + 5; // Closure is
assigned to 'add_five'

println!("{}", add_five(3)); // Output: 8
```

- |num: i32| num + 5 is the closure.
- It "closes over" its environment, having access to any variables declared in that context.

Key Points about Closures

- **Syntax:** |parameters| expression
- **Inferred Types:** Rust usually infers the types of closure parameters and the return type.
- **Capturing Environment:**

- Fn: Borrows by reference (&)
- FnMut : Borrows mutably (&mut)
- FnOnce: Takes ownership

Superpower: Higher-Order Functions

Closures shine when combined with functions that take other functions as arguments. Let's rewrite a generic "apply" function:

```
fn apply<F>(list: Vec<i32>, func: F) -> Vec<i32>
 where F: Fn(i32) -> i32 {
    list.into_iter().map(func).collect()
}

fn main() {
    let numbers = vec![1, 2, 3];
    let doubled = apply(numbers, |x| x * 2);
    println!("{:?}", doubled);
}
```

Common Use-Cases of Closures

- **Iterators:** The `.map`, `.filter`, `.fold`, and similar methods on iterators all use closures.
- **Custom Sorting:**`Vec::sort_by` lets you provide a closure as the comparison function.
- **Callbacks:** For event handling in asynchronous code or GUIs, closures are often used to define actions to take when events occur.

Closures vs. Regular Functions

- **Flexibility:** Closures can be created on the fly, right where they're needed.
- **Capturing Context:** Closures bundle both code and necessary data.
- **Trade-off:** For larger, reusable functions, named functions (`fn`) are generally a better choice due to readability and clarity.

Next: Extending Closures + Traits

We'll see how to make closures even more flexible, explore more functional patterns, and the interplay between closures and Rust's powerful traits.

Additional Resources

- **Closures in the Rust Book:**
  https://doc.rust-lang.org/book/ch13-01-closures.html

Tip: Experiment! Try converting small imperative code chunks into equivalents using closures and higher-order functions like map and filter.

_____

_____

_____

Extending Closures: Advanced Strategies for Functional Programming in Rust

Traits + Closures = Superpowers

Remember traits like `Iterator`? Their methods (`map`, `filter`, etc.) heavily rely on closures under the hood. Let's implement a simplified 'find' to see how:

```rust
trait MyIterator<T> {
    fn my_find<F>(&self, predicate: F) -> Option<&T>
    where F: FnMut(&T) -> bool;
}

// (Simplified) Implementation on Vec:
impl<T> MyIterator<T> for Vec<T> {
    fn my_find<F>(&self, predicate: F) -> Option<&T>
    where F: FnMut(&T) -> bool {
        for item in self {
```

```
            if predicate(item) { // Calling the
closure!
                return Some(item);
            }
        }
        None
    }
}
```

Let's use it:

```
let numbers = vec![5, 10, 3, 15];
let first_even = numbers.my_find(|num| num % 2 ==
0);
```

Returning Closures

Functions can even return other closures, enabling techniques like currying (breaking functions into a series taking one argument at a time):

```
fn create_multiplier(factor: i32) -> impl Fn(i32) ->
i32 {
    move |x| x * factor  // Closure 'captures' the
'factor'
}
```

```
let multiply_by_10 = create_multiplier(10);
println!("{}", multiply_by_10(5));
```

Caution: Closures and Lifetimes

When closures capture variables by reference, you need to be mindful of lifetimes to avoid errors, since the closure might outlive the data it references.

Functional Programming in Action

Let's rewrite a task filtering function in our hypothetical "Rusty ToDo List" using functional techniques:

```
// Before:
fn get_incomplete_tasks(tasks: &Vec<Task>) ->
Vec<Task> {
    let mut result = Vec::new();
    for task in tasks {
        if !task.is_completed() {
            result.push(task.clone());
        }
    }
    result
}


// After (more concise and functional):
fn get_incomplete_tasks(tasks: &Vec<Task>) ->
Vec<Task> {
    tasks.iter()
        .filter(|task| !task.is_completed())
        .cloned() // Note: 'cloned' needed if tasks
are not Copy
        .collect()
}
```

Next Up: Concurrency Time!

We're about to venture into the world of concurrency in Rust – writing code that can perform multiple tasks in a seemingly parallel fashion, unlocking performance on modern multi-core systems.

Additional Resources

- **The Iterator Trait in Rust**
  https://doc.rust-lang.org/std/iter/trait.Iterator.html

Exploring Threads: Concurrency in Rust, Part 1

What is Concurrency?

- **Concurrency** is about structuring your program to have multiple tasks seemingly progressing at the same time. This is not always true parallelism (which requires multiple cores).
- **Think of:** A web server handling multiple requests simultaneously, or a GUI application keeping the interface responsive while doing a heavy calculation.

Why Concurrency Matters

- **Performance:** Utilize multiple cores for computationally intensive work.
- **Responsiveness:** Prevent a long-running task from blocking user interaction.
- **Managing Asynchronous Operations:** I/O (disk, network) can be handled with concurrent workflows.

Introducing Threads in Rust

Rust's primary way to achieve concurrency is using OS threads, provided by the standard library:

```rust
use std::thread;
use std::time::Duration;

fn main() {
    let handle = thread::spawn(|| {   // Spawning a new thread
        for i in 1..5 {
            println!("Count from thread: {}", i);

thread::sleep(Duration::from_millis(500));
        }
    });
```

```
    // Main thread continues here
    println!("This is the main thread speaking");

    handle.join().unwrap(); // Waits for the thread
to finish
}
```

Communicating Between Threads

Rust provides safe ways to share data between threads:

- **Channels:** Think of them as pipes. You have a sender and receiver. (`std::sync::mpsc`)
- **Mutex:** Enforces "mutual exclusion". Allows only one thread at a time to access a shared resource (`std::sync::Mutex`)
- **Arc:** Atomic Reference Counter. For sharing ownership of data across threads (`std::sync::Arc`)

A Word of Caution: Data Races

Concurrency introduces the risk of data races – multiple threads accessing/modifying the same data simultaneously, leading to unpredictable bugs. Rust's ownership and borrowing help prevent many data race scenarios at compile time!

Up Next: Advanced Concurrency

In the next chapter, we'll go deeper, exploring synchronization primitives, the perils of deadlocks, and the elegant solutions Rust offers for safe and fearless concurrent programming.

Additional Resources

- **Threads in the Rust Book:**
  https://doc.rust-lang.org/book/ch16-01-threads.html
- **The `std::thread` module documentation:**
  https://doc.rust-lang.org/std/thread/index.html

Concurrency Mastery: Advanced Techniques for Multi-Threading in Rust, Part 2

Advanced Synchronization Tools

- **Mutex Revisited:** While a `Mutex` allows single-thread access to data, it can lead to deadlocks if not used carefully. Consider alternatives like `RwLock` (Read-Write Lock) when multiple threads need read access concurrently.
- **Atomic Types:** For simple counters or updates, `std::sync::atomic` provides built-in types for thread-safe modifications without the need for explicit locking.
- **Condition Variables (`Condvar`):** Allow threads to wait for a specific condition to be true and get notified when it changes, useful for complex task coordination.

Managing Deadlocks

A deadlock occurs when two or more threads are stuck waiting on resources held by each other. Strategies to reduce or prevent them:

- **Lock Ordering:** Establish a consistent order in which threads acquire locks.
- **Timeouts:** Have threads try to acquire locks with a timeout, recovering gracefully if they fail.
- **"Lock-free" Data Structures:** Highly specialized, but some concurrent data structures avoid classic locks altogether.

Beyond Basics: Fearless Concurrency

Rust's type system and the powerful Send and Sync traits come to the rescue:

- **Send:** A type is Send if it can be safely moved between threads.
- **Sync:** A type is Sync if it can be safely shared between threads (&T is safe).

The compiler enforces these rules, preventing many common concurrency bugs at compile-time!

Parallel Iterators with Rayon

The Rayon library makes turning sequential iterators into parallel ones incredibly easy:

```
use rayon::prelude::*;

let mut numbers = vec![1, 2, 3, 4];

numbers.par_iter_mut()
        .for_each(|num| *num *= 10);
```

Choosing the Right Approach

- **Need Shared State?** Channels, `Mutex`, `Arc`, etc. are the way to go.
- **Data-Parallel Tasks?** Rayon simplifies parallel work.
- **Asynchronous Programming?** Rust's `async`/`await` features (beyond the immediate scope of this book) provide a structured approach for concurrency driven by events.

Up Next: Let's Build a Project!

Our hands-on journey continues. We'll apply your newfound knowledge to build a simple To-do list application using Rust, "Rusty ToDo List".

Additional Resources

- **Atomic Types in Rust:** https://doc.rust-lang.org/std/sync/atomic/
- **The Rayon Crate:** https://docs.rs/rayon/
- **Fearless Concurrency with Rust Blog Post:** https://blog.rust-lang.org/2015/04/10/Fearless-Concurrency.html

Tip: Profile your multi-threaded application to identify potential bottlenecks or unnecessary thread synchronization overheads.

Section 5:

Hands-On Project - Rusty ToDo List (A simple command-line ToDo list application)

Setting Up the Project

In this chapter, we'll prepare the foundation for our "Rusty ToDo List" command-line application. You'll set up the necessary project structure, create the primary Rust file, and get everything ready to start coding our task management system.

Objectives

By the end of this chapter, you will have:

- Created a new Rust project using Cargo.
- Installed any essential dependencies for the project.
- Set up a basic file structure for organizing your code.

Let's Get Started

1. **Creating a Cargo Project:**
   - Open your terminal or command prompt.
   - Navigate to a suitable directory where you want to create your project. For instance:

```
cd ~/Documents/RustProjects
```

○ Use Cargo to initialize a new Rust project:

```
cargo new rusty_todo_list
```

○ This creates a new directory called `rusty_todo_list` with these essential files:
- `Cargo.toml`: The project configuration file.
- `src/main.rs`: Your Rust source code.

2. **Installing Dependencies:**
Our initial project won't need extensive external libraries. However, it's good practice to list any future dependencies in your `Cargo.toml` file. For later chapters, we might consider crates (Rust packages) for features like colored terminal output or file handling.
You can find suitable crates by exploring https://crates.io/.

3. **Structuring Your Project:**
○ Inside the `src` directory of your project, it's helpful for larger projects to organize your code into modules. Create a file named `todo.rs` alongside your `main.rs`. We'll develop our task management logic within this file.

Your Project Structure

Your project directory should look like this:

```
rusty_todo_list/
├── Cargo.toml
└── src/
    ├── main.rs
    └── todo.rs
```

Setting Up the Basic Code

1. Open `src/main.rs` in your code editor.
2. Add the following code:

```
mod todo; // Import our task management module

fn main() {
    println!("Rusty ToDo List - Project Setup
Complete!");
}
```

Testing Your Setup

Run the following command in your terminal (from within the `rusty_todo_list` directory):

```
cargo run
```

You should see "Rusty ToDo List - Project Setup Complete!" printed on your console.

Additional Resources

- **The Rust Programming Language Book - Cargo:** https://doc.rust-lang.org/book/ch01-03-hello-cargo.html
- **Crates.io:** https://crates.io/

Let's Move On

With your project foundation set, you're ready to dive into the core of our To-Do list application. In the next chapter, we'll tackle defining a task structure and start creating and displaying tasks!

Creating and Displaying Tasks

Now that your project foundation is laid, let's breathe life into our ToDo list! In this chapter, you'll learn how to represent tasks in Rust, enable users to add new tasks, and neatly display the existing task list.

Objectives

- Define a Task struct to store task information.
- Implement functionality to create new task instances.
- Store the tasks in a suitable data structure.
- Display the current list of tasks to the user.

Representing Tasks with Structs

1. Open your todo.rs file.
2. Inside this file, define a struct to represent a task:

```rust
struct Task {
    description: String,
    completed: bool,
}
```

- The description field is a String to hold the task's text description.
- The completed field is a bool (boolean) flag that's true if a task is finished and false otherwise.

Creating New Tasks

Let's implement a function to create new Task instances:

```rust
impl Task { // Implement methods associated with the
Task struct
    pub fn new(description: String) -> Task {
        Task {
            description,
            completed: false,
        }
    }
}
```

- The new function is a constructor, conventionally used to create instances of structs.

- It takes a `description` string and creates a `Task` with the completed flag initially set to `false`.

Storing Tasks

In `main.rs`, we'll store tasks in a vector:

```rust
use todo::Task; // Import the Task struct

fn main() {
    let mut todo_list: Vec<Task> = Vec::new(); //
Create a vector to hold tasks

    // ... rest of your setup code ...
}
```

Getting User Input

We'll use standard input to let users add tasks:

```rust
use std::io;

fn main() {
    // ... (your existing code) ...

    println!("Enter a new task: ");
    let mut task_description = String::new();
    io::stdin().read_line(&mut
task_description).expect("Failed to read input");

    let new_task =
Task::new(task_description.trim().to_string()); //
Create task
    todo_list.push(new_task); // Add task to the
list
}
```

Displaying the Task List

Let's write a simple function to display tasks:

```rust
fn display_tasks(todo_list: &Vec<Task>) { // 
Function to display tasks
    if todo_list.is_empty() {
        println!("Your task list is empty!");
    } else {
        println!("Task List:");
        for (index, task) in
todo_list.iter().enumerate() {
            println!("{}: {} (Completed: {})", index
+ 1, task.description, task.completed);
        }
    }
}
```

Putting It All Together (in `main.rs`)

```rust
// ... (imports, setup, input code from above) ...

display_tasks(&todo_list);  // Display the updated
task list
```

Additional Resources

- **Structs in Rust:**
  https://doc.rust-lang.org/book/ch05-01-defining-structs.html
- **Vectors in Rust:** https://doc.rust-lang.org/std/vec/
- **Rust Standard Input:** https://doc.rust-lang.org/std/io/

Updating and Deleting Tasks

In the previous chapter, we laid the groundwork for creating tasks. Now, let's give our ToDo list true flexibility by allowing users to modify and remove existing tasks.

Objectives

- Enable users to select a task by its index number.
- Implement functionality to mark a task as 'completed'.
- Allow users to delete tasks from the list.

Selecting Tasks

We'll need a way to let users choose the task they want to interact with. Here's a simple approach using task indexes:

1. **Display the task list with numbered indexes** (you likely already have this from the previous chapter)
2. **Get user input** to specify the index of the task they want to modify.

Marking Tasks as Completed

1. Add a method to the Task struct to toggle the `completed` status:

```rust
impl Task {

    // ... (your existing methods) ...



    pub fn toggle_completion(&mut self) {

        self.completed = !self.completed;

    }

}
```

2. Modify your `main.rs` to do the following after getting the task index from the user:

```
// ... (Get user input for task selection) ...


if let Some(task) = todo_list.get_mut(task_index
- 1) { // Adjust for indexing

    task.toggle_completion();

    println!("Task marked as completed!");

} else {

    println!("Invalid task index.");

}
```

Deleting Tasks

1. In main.rs, get the task index to delete like before.
2. Use the vector's remove method:

```
// ... (Get user input for task deletion) ...


if task_index - 1 < todo_list.len() {

    todo_list.remove(task_index - 1);

    println!("Task deleted!");

} else {

    println!("Invalid task index.");

}
```

Complete Example (Updating `main.rs`)

Here's a more complete look at how you might structure parts of your `main.rs`:

```rust
// ... (imports, setup, etc.) ...


loop { // Example: A simple input loop for actions

    println!("Enter action (add, complete,
delete):");

    let mut action = String::new();

    io::stdin().read_line(&mut
action).expect("Failed to read input");


    match action.trim().to_lowercase().as_str() {
// Match on the action

        "add" => {

            // ... (Your code to add a task from
previous chapter) ...

        }

        "complete" => {

            display_tasks(&todo_list);

            // ... (Code to get task index, mark as
complete) ...

        }

        "delete" => {

            display_tasks(&todo_list);
```

```
                // ... (Code to get task index, delete
the task) ...

        }

        _ => println!("Invalid action"),

    }

}
```

Additional Resources

- **Methods in Rust Structs:**
  https://doc.rust-lang.org/book/ch05-03-method-syntax.html
- **Match expressions in Rust:**
  https://doc.rust-lang.org/book/ch06-02-match.html

Enhancements

- **Error Handling:** Consider using Rust's Result type and error handling mechanisms for a more robust program.
- **Menu:** Create a clear menu-driven interface for better user experience.

Next Up

We're progressing well! Next, we'll tackle saving your task list to a file so users don't lose their progress when the program ends.

Saving and Loading Tasks from a File

Up until now, our ToDo list vanishes when the program closes. Let's change that! In this chapter, you'll learn how to preserve your tasks between sessions by saving them to a file and loading them back when the application starts.

102

Objectives

- Choose a suitable file format for storing your task data.
- Implement code to serialize tasks into the chosen format.
- Write functions to save the serialized data to a file.
- Load the file and deserialize the task data.

Choosing a File Format

Several choices work well for this project:

- **Plain Text:** Easy to read and modify. You could define a simple custom format.
- **JSON:** Structured format, straightforward to work with in many languages.
- **TOML:** Similar to JSON, designed for configuration files.
- **YAML:** Human-readable data format.

We'll use JSON for its widespread support and readability.

Serialization with Serde

Rust's powerful `serde` crate makes serialization and deserialization smooth.

1. **Add Dependency:** Add `serde`, `serde_derive`, and `serde_json` to the dependencies section of your `Cargo.toml`.
2. **Deriving Traits:** Modify your `Task` struct to support `serde`:

```
#[derive(Serialize, Deserialize)] // Add this
line
struct Task {
    description: String,
    completed: bool,
}
```

Saving Tasks

```
use std::fs::File;
```

```rust
use std::io::Write;

fn save_tasks(todo_list: &Vec<Task>, filename: &str)
-> Result<(), std::io::Error> {
    let serialized_tasks =
serde_json::to_string(todo_list)?; // Serialize
tasks to JSON
    let mut file = File::create(filename)?;
    file.write_all(serialized_tasks.as_bytes())?;

    Ok(())
}
```

Loading Tasks

```rust
use std::fs::read_to_string;

fn load_tasks(filename: &str) -> Result<Vec<Task>,
std::io::Error> {
    let contents = read_to_string(filename)?;
    let tasks: Vec<Task> =
serde_json::from_str(&contents)?;  // Deserialize
JSON
    Ok(tasks)
}
```

Integrating into `main.rs`

- **On Start:** Attempt to load the task list from a file (e.g., "todo.json"). If the file doesn't exist, that's fine; just start with an empty list.
- **On Exit (or Save Action):** Call the `save_tasks` function to preserve changes.

Additional Resources

- **The Serde Crate:** https://serde.rs/
- **File I/O in Rust:** https://doc.rust-lang.org/std/fs/

- **JSON in Rust:** https://docs.serde.rs/serde_json/

Tip: Choose a descriptive name for your save file (e.g., "todo_list.json")

Challenges & Enhancements

- **Error Handling:** Consider how to gracefully handle situations where the file cannot be loaded or saved and inform the user.
- **Data Validation:** You might want to sanitize and validate data loaded from the file.

Next Steps

With the persistence layer in place, let's move on to enriching your ToDo application further by allowing users to set priorities and due dates for their tasks!

Adding Priority and Due Date Functionality

Let's empower our ToDo list by giving tasks a sense of urgency and timeline. In this chapter, you'll learn how to incorporate priorities and due dates into your task management system.

Objectives

- Modify the Task struct to store priority and due date information.
- Implement functionality for users to set and view these attributes.
- Consider how to display and sort tasks based on priority and due dates.

Modifying the Task Struct

We'll need to add fields to the Task struct. You have a few options:

- **Priority:**
  - You could use an enum (e.g., enum `Priority { Low, Medium, High }`).
  - Alternatively, a simple integer representing priority level works fine too.
- **Due Date:**
  - A naive approach is to store it as a `String`.
  - For more sophisticated date handling, consider the `chrono` crate: https://docs.rs/chrono

Example update to the struct:

```rust
use chrono::NaiveDate; // If you choose to use the
'chrono' crate

struct Task {
    description: String,
    completed: bool,
    priority: i32,              // 1 for low, 2 for
medium, etc.
    due_date: Option<NaiveDate>, // Optional to
allow tasks without due dates
}
```

Getting Input for Priority & Due Date

You'll need to expand your user input mechanisms in `main.rs` to collect priority and due date when creating tasks. Here's a basic example (assuming the simple integer priority approach):

```rust
println!("Enter task priority (e.g., 1 for low):");
let mut priority_str = String::new();
io::stdin().read_line(&mut
priority_str).expect("Failed to read input");
let priority: i32 =
priority_str.trim().parse().expect("Invalid
priority");
```

Displaying with Priorities and Due Dates

Update your `display_tasks` function to present the new information:

```rust
fn display_tasks(todo_list: &Vec<Task>) {
    // ... your existing display code ...

    for (index, task) in
todo_list.iter().enumerate() {
        println!("{}: {} (Completed: {}, Priority:
{}, Due: {})",
                index + 1,
                task.description,
                task.completed,
                task.priority,

task.due_date.map_or("None".to_string(), |date|
date.format("%Y-%m-%d").to_string()) // Handle due
date formatting
        );
    }
}
```

Enhancements

- **Sorting:** Add features to sort the task list by priority or due date (ascending or descending), giving users various ways to view their list.
- **Due Date Input:** Implement robust parsing and validation of user-provided due dates.
- **Overdue Notifications:** You could highlight tasks that are past their due date.

Additional Resources

- **Rust Enums:** https://doc.rust-lang.org/book/ch06-01-defining-an-enum.html
- **Chrono Crate:** https://docs.rs/chrono

Next Steps

With priority and due date functionality, your ToDo list app is even more practical. Next, let's give the app a visual overhaul by adding color and styling to the terminal interface!

Adding Color and Styling to the Interface

Let's breathe some life into our text-based ToDo list by adding color and other styling elements. A visually appealing interface can significantly improve the user experience.

Objectives

- Introduce a library for handling terminal colors and styling.
- Apply colors to distinguish task states (completed vs. pending).
- Use styling techniques (e.g., bold, underline) to emphasize important information.

Choosing a Library

Several Rust crates can help with terminal styling. We'll use the popular `colored` crate:

> **Add Dependency:** Update your `Cargo.toml` file:

```
[dependencies]
colored = "2.1.0"
```

Styling Your Output

Let's modify the `display_tasks` function to make use of colors:

```
use colored::*; // Import the 'colored' crate
```

```
fn display_tasks(todo_list: &Vec<Task>) {
    // ... your existing display code ...

    for (index, task) in
todo_list.iter().enumerate() {
        let status_color = if task.completed {
"green" } else { "red" };

        println!("{}: {} (Completed: {}, Priority:
{}, Due: {})",
                index + 1,
                task.description,

task.completed.to_string().color(status_color), //
Color for status
                task.priority,

task.due_date.map_or("None".to_string(), |date|
date.format("%Y-%m-%d").to_string())
        );
    }
}
```

Beyond Basics

The `colored` crate gives you much more:

- **Text Styles:** Use `.bold()`, `.underline()`, `.italic()`, and
  more.
- **RGB Colors:** For custom colors, use `.truecolor(R, G, B)`

Example: Highlight Overdue Tasks

```
// ... inside your task display loop ...
let due_date_display = if let Some(due_date) =
task.due_date {
    if due_date <
chrono::Local::today().naive_local() {
```

```
due_date.format("%Y-%m-%d").to_string().color("red")
.bold() // Overdue!
    } else {
        due_date.format("%Y-%m-%d").to_string()
    }
} else {
    "None".to_string()
};

println!("... (Due: {})", due_date_display);
```

Additional Resources

- **The colored Crate:** https://docs.rs/colored/
- **More Terminal Styling Options (if you're curious):** Try crates like `termion`, `crossterm`, or `tui-rs`.

Important Considerations

- **Cross-Platform:** Not all terminals support advanced styling or colors in the same way. Test if possible.
- **User Preferences:** Consider allowing users to customize the color scheme or perhaps toggle styling on or off.

Next Steps

Your ToDo list is looking sharp! In our final chapter, let's focus on writing tests and refactoring your code to ensure the long-term quality and maintainability of your application.

Testing and Refactoring

As your ToDo list application grows, ensuring its correctness and making changes without breaking things becomes crucial. In this chapter, you'll learn how to write tests to safeguard your code's behavior and refactor to improve its structure for long-term success.

Objectives

- Understand the basics of writing unit tests in Rust.
- Write tests for core functions in your ToDo list project.
- Introduce refactoring techniques to enhance code readability and maintainability.

Rust's Built-in Testing

Rust has excellent testing support baked right in. Here's how to get started:

1. **Test Functions:** Annotate test functions with the #[test] attribute.
2. **Assertions:** Use assert!, assert_eq!, and related macros to verify conditions within your tests.

Example Test for Task Completion

```
mod tests { // Create a 'tests' module
    use super::*; // Import your ToDo list code

    #[test]
    fn task_toggle_completion() {
        let mut task = Task::new("Sample task".to_string());
        assert!(!task.completed); // Initially incomplete

        task.toggle_completion();
        assert!(task.completed); // Now completed
    }
}
```

Testing in Your Project

Focus on testing these key areas of your "Rusty ToDo List":

- **Task Struct Functionality:**
  - Verify that creation, completion toggling, priority setting (if applicable), etc., work as expected.
- **Input Handling:**
  - Test your code that gets user input for correct behavior, including error handling for invalid inputs.
- **File Operations:**
  - Ensure saving and loading tasks to and from your file format operate correctly.

Refactoring: Improving Code Without Changing Behavior

As your project evolves, you'll want to restructure your code to keep it organized and adaptable. Here are some common refactoring techniques:

- **Extract Functions:** Break down large functions into smaller, well-defined functions (`update_task`, `display_overdue_tasks`, etc.). This improves modularity and testability.
- **Rename Variables:** Use descriptive variable names to enhance code readability.
- **Simplify Logic:** Look for ways to streamline `if-else` chains or complex expressions for better clarity.

Example Refactoring

You might have a large chunk of code within `main.rs` that handles all user interactions. Refactor parts of it into functions:

```
fn display_menu() { /* ... your menu display code
... */ }


fn get_user_action() -> String { /* ... get and
return the action ... */ }
```

```
fn handle_add_task(todo_list: &mut Vec<Task>) { /*
... task creation logic ... */ }

// ... more functions for other actions …
```

Additional Resources

- **The Rust Book (Testing Chapter):**
  https://doc.rust-lang.org/book/ch11-00-testing.html

Continuous Improvement

- **Test-Driven Development (TDD):** Consider adopting TDD, where you write tests before the implementation code.
- **Code Coverage:** Explore tools that measure how much of your code is covered by tests.

Conclusion

Congratulations! You've embarked on a remarkable journey through the world of Rust programming. From Cargo's navigation to mastering traits and concurrency, you've built a robust foundation in a language designed for reliability, speed, and fearless development.

The Power of Rust at Your Fingertips

Remember, Rust empowers you to tackle diverse challenges:

- **Systems Programming:** Craft low-level systems, network utilities, or embed Rust into other languages.
- **Web Development:** Explore frameworks like Rocket for blazingly fast and secure web applications.

- **Game Development:** Harness engines like Amethyst or Bevy to create the next captivating gaming experiences.
- **Blockchain and WebAssembly:** Contribute to the future of decentralized applications and browser-based environments.

A Community of Builders

Don't forget, you're not alone! The Rust community is welcoming and always eager to help. Participate in online forums, share your projects, and continue enriching your knowledge. The best part is that Rust's stability and commitment to backward compatibility ensure that the skills you've gained will hold value for years to come.

Continuing the Adventure

Your Rust journey has just begun. Keep these practices in mind as you venture forward:

- **Embrace Project-Based Learning:** Strengthen your skills by building increasingly complex applications.
- **Explore the Crate Ecosystem:** Leverage the rich resources on https://crates.io/ for powerful, well-tested libraries.
- **Contribute:** Give back to the community by sharing code, writing documentation, or helping others.

The Future is Yours to Build

The realm of possibilities with Rust is vast. Whether seeking to optimize existing systems, innovate in emerging technologies, or simply craft elegant and efficient software – Rust is your powerful companion. Seize the opportunities, and let your creativity soar!

Additional Resources to Stay Sharp

- **The Rust Programming Language (Official Website):** https://www.rust-lang.org/
- **The Rust Blog:** https://blog.rust-lang.org/
- **This Week in Rust Newsletter:** https://this-week-in-rust.org/

Thank you for joining this fast-track guide. Go forth, and build amazing things with Rust!

www.ingramcontent.com/pod-product-compliance
Lightning Source LLC
Chambersburg PA
CBHW080539060326
40690CB00022B/5178